# TOUCH PAPERS

# TOUCH PAPERS

## Dialogues on Touch in the Psychoanalytic Space

Edited by

*Graeme Galton*

With foreword by Susie Orbach

**KARNAC**

First published in 2006 by
Karnac Books Ltd.
118 Finchley Road, London NW3 5HT

Chapter Three is a revised and updated version of a previous paper,
originally published in the *Journal of Analytical Psychology*, 15(1): 1970,
pp. 42–58. Reprinted with permission.

"Caught Out" is printed with thanks to Bradgate Poetry Press.

British Library Cataloguing in Publication Data

A C.I.P. for this book is available from the British Library

ISBN-10: 1 85575 445 2
ISBN-13: 978 1 85575 445 4

Edited, designed and produced by The Studio Publishing Services Ltd,
www.studiopublishingservicesuk.co.uk
e-mail: studio@publishingservices.co.uk

Printed in Great Britain

10 9 8 7 6 5 4 3 2 1

www.karnacbooks.com

# CONTENTS

ABOUT THE EDITOR AND CONTRIBUTORS     vii

FOREWORD *by Susie Orbach*     xiii

INTRODUCTION *by Graeme Galton*     xix

CHAPTER ONE
Winnicott's experiments with physical contact: creative innovation
or chaotic impingement?
    *Brett Kahr*     1

CHAPTER TWO
Touching and affective closeness
    *A. H. Brafman*     15

CHAPTER THREE
Symbolic understanding of tactile communication
in psychotherapy
    *Camilla Bosanquet*     29

CHAPTER FOUR
*No touch please*—we're British psychodynamic practitioners
    *Valerie Sinason*     49

CHAPTER FIVE
Can touching be relevant to understanding some patients
in psychoanalysis?
   *Pearl King*                                                        61

CHAPTER SIX
Bearing witness to an abused patient's physical injuries
   *Graeme Galton*                                                     69

CHAPTER SEVEN
Between touches
   *Nicola Diamond*                                                    79

CHAPTER EIGHT
The presence of the body in psychotherapy
   *Em Farrell*                                                        97

CHAPTER NINE
The issue of physical contact in psychoanalytic work with
children and adolescents
   *Maria Emilia Pozzi*                                               109

CHAPTER TEN
Strong adaptive perspectives on patient–therapist
physical contact
   *Robert Langs*                                                     123

CHAPTER ELEVEN
A body psychotherapist's approach to touch
   *Nick Totton*                                                      145

CHAPTER TWELVE
Something dangerous: touch in forensic practice
   *Emma Ramsden, Angela Pryor, Sarita Bose,*
   *Sharmila Charles, and Gwen Adshead*                               163

REFERENCES                                                            179

INDEX                                                                 189

**Camilla Bosanquet** is a Jungian analyst and professional member of the Society of Analytical Psychology, where she is a past chairman and training analyst. Before training as a Jungian analyst, she qualified in medicine, working as a General Practitioner and then as a psychiatrist in the National Health Service. She later worked as a psychotherapist at University College Hospital in London and London School of Economics, while also maintaining a private practice. She is a founder member of the Guild of Psychotherapists.

**A. H. Brafman** is a psychoanalyst of adults and children and worked in the National Health Service as a Consultant Child and Adolescent Psychiatrist. He has been involved in teaching programmes for analysts and therapists and was a member of the Ethics Committee of the British Association of Psychotherapists. He is also an Honorary Senior Lecturer at the Psychotherapy Department of University College Hospital in London, teaching medical students during their psychiatry placement. His books include *Untying the Knot: Working with Children and Parents* and *Can You Help Me? A Guide for Parents*.

**Nicola Diamond** is the Director of PhD studies at the School of Psychotherapy and Counselling at Regent's College, London, and is a psychoanalytic psychotherapist (British Association of Psychotherapists) in private practice. She has worked with children, adolescents, and adults in the National Health Service, and is one of the founding members of the International Attachment Network. Her specialized area of interest is the body. She is co-author, with Mario Marrone, of *Attachment and Intersubjectivity*.

**Em Farrell** is a psychodynamic psychotherapist and supervisor in private practice. She teaches on a number of psychotherapy trainings and runs workshops on eating disorders for practitioners, as well as running body image workshops for children in schools. She has written a book on the psychoanalytic psychotherapy of eating disorders, *Lost for Words: The Psychoanalysis of Anorexia and Bulimia*.

**Graeme Galton** was born in Australia and lives in London. He is a psychoanalytic psychotherapist in the National Health Service and in private practice. At the Parkside Clinic in London he works with individuals and groups in an NHS outpatient psychotherapy service. He also works at the Clinic for Dissociative Studies, a small specialist outpatient mental health service for people suffering from severe trauma and dissociation. He is a registered member of the Centre for Attachment-based Psychoanalytic Psychotherapy, where he is a training supervisor and teaches on the clinical training programme. He is also a visiting tutor at the School of Psychotherapy and Counselling, Regent's College, London.

**Brett Kahr** is Senior Clinical Research Fellow in Psychotherapy and Mental Health at the Centre for Child Mental Health, London, and the Winnicott Clinic Senior Research Fellow in Psychotherapy. He is also Senior Lecturer in Psychotherapy in the School of Psychotherapy and Counselling at Regent's College, London and Visiting Clinician at the Tavistock Centre for Couple Relationships. He is the author of several books, including *D. W. Winnicott: A Biographical Portrait*, which won the Gradiva Award for Biography, as well as *Forensic Psychotherapy and Psychopathology: Winnicottian Perspectives*, *The Legacy of Winnicott: Essays on Infant and Child Mental Health*, as well as a book on *Exhibitionism*. He has recently been appointed as

Resident Psychotherapist for BBC Radio 2. He works in private practice as a psychoanalytic psychotherapist and marital psychotherapist.

**Pearl King** is an Honorary Member and a training and supervising psychoanalyst of the British Psychoanalytical Society and an Honorary Member of the Finnish Psychoanalytical Society. She was formerly President of the British Psychoanalytical Society, Honorary Secretary of the International Psychoanalytical Association and Honorary Archivist to the British Psychoanalytical Society. She is co-editor, with Riccardo Steiner, of *The Freud/Klein Controversies 1941–1945*, and has edited and compiled a selection of John Rickman's papers, *No Ordinary Psychoanalyst: The Exceptional Contributions of John Rickman*, which contains her biography of Rickman. She recently published a selection of her own papers, *Time Present and Time Past*. In 1992 she received the Sigourney Award for outstanding contributions to psychoanalysis.

**Robert Langs** works in private practice as a psychoanalyst in New York. He is an Honorary Visiting Fellow at the School of Psychotherapy and Counselling at Regent's College in London. He is the author of forty-three books and over 150 scientific papers and book chapters. His many books have sold more than one million copies and include *Doing Supervision and Being Supervised; Dreams and Emotional Adaptation; Ground Rules in Psychotherapy and Counselling; Death Anxiety in Clinical Practice;* and *Fundamentals of Adaptive Psychotherapy and Counselling*.

**Susie Orbach** PhD, is the Co-Founder, The Women's Therapy Centre (1976), and Visiting Professor at the London School of Economics. She is the author of *Fat is a Feminist Issue* (Paddington, 1978); *Understanding Women* (Penguin, 1982); *Hunger Strike* (Faber, 1986); *Between Women* (Penguin, 1987); *The Impossibility of Sex* (Penguin, 1999); *Towards Emotional Literacy* (Virago, 1999); and *On Eating* (Penguin, 2001).

**Maria Emilia Pozzi** was born in Italy and trained as a child and adolescent psychotherapist at the Tavistock Clinic, then as an adult psychotherapist with the British Association of Psychotherapists.

She is a Visiting Tutor at the Tavistock Clinic, the British Association of Psychotherapists, and the London Centre for Psychotherapy. She also teaches and lectures in Italy and Switzerland on topics related to child and adolescent psychotherapy. She has special interests in treating children with autism, Asperger's syndrome, and mental handicap and in brief work with children under five and their families. Her publications include the book *Psychic Hooks and Bolts: Psychoanalytic Work with Children Under Five and their Families.*

**Emma Ramsden, Angela Pryor, Sarita Bose, Sharmila Charles, and Gwen Adshead** are all forensic therapists at Broadmoor Hospital in Berkshire. Emma Ramsden is a drama therapist who has developed a group work intervention for sex offender treatment in the hospital. Angela Pryor is a speech and language therapist who has a particular interest in forensic mental health and language. Sarita Bose and Sharmila Charles are nurse therapists working in the structured group work programme developed by the Psychology Department at Broadmoor Hospital. Gwen Adshead is a psychiatrist and psychotherapist who has written and edited several books, including *Ethical Issues in Forensic Mental Health Research,* which she co-edited with Christine Brown.

**Valerie Sinason** is a child and adult psychotherapist and an adult psychoanalyst. She is Director of the Clinic for Dissociative Studies and a Consultant Research Psychotherapist in the Psychiatry of Disability Department at St George's Hospital Medical School, in London. She is a poet and writer and has published thirteen books and over seventy professional papers, mainly on learning disability and abuse. Her books include *Mental Handicap and the Human Condition; Treating Survivors of Satanist Abuse; Memory in Dispute;* and *Attachment, Trauma and Multiplicity: Working with Dissociative Identity Disorder.* She has also published two volumes of poetry entitled *Inkstains & Stilettos* and *Night Shift.*

**Nick Totton** is a psychotherapist and trainer in private practice based in Calderdale, West Yorkshire. Originally trained in post Reichian therapy, over the last twenty-odd years he has developed (originally in collaboration with Em Edmondson) the form of work which he now practises and teaches, Embodied–Relational Therapy.

He is the author of several books, including *The Water in the Glass: Body and Mind in Psychoanalysis*; *Psychotherapy and Politics*; *Body Psychotherapy: An Introduction*; and *Press When Illuminated: New and Selected Poems*. He edits the journal *Psychotherapy and Politics International*.

# Too hot to touch?

*Susie Orbach*

Several assumptions dominate the discourse on touch in psycho-analysis. The first is that it is wrong, inappropriate, and unsafe: touch initiated by the therapist is invasive, potentially transgres-sive, and may bypass important psychic material. Another assump-tion is that when touch occurs it is because the patient has regressed and that a developmental deficit has brought it into the therapy. Yet another assumption is to see touch as a one-off occurrence that was either unfortunate, that worked in this particular instance, or was a close shave.

Such assumptions are so embedded in psychoanalytic thinking about touch that we have a very sparse literature on touch within the therapy relationship. Further, there is an idea that since all agree that touch is not a good idea, there is very little to discuss. The essays in this collection, including, as they do, those who work with children—who, of course, do not know the unwritten rules of therapy and thus do leap on one, cuddle up spontaneously, hug or kick—and therapists who work directly with touch in body therapy, are an attempt to open up a space in which the issues around touch can be thought about afresh.

Of course, it may well be the case that we do all more or less agree about the taboo on touch. But I don't see how we could be sure, since we have no systematic way to explore our thoughts about the topic. Through our training we absorb canonical knowledge without being able to interrogate it sufficiently. Perhaps we are surprised when we first learn of the taboo on touch. We can find it hard to get our head around the idea, but with a few judicious illustrations showing the negative impact of touch we bow to what we as neophytes don't know, and for the most part we accept what we are learning. Perhaps we are relieved. A door closed. Something we can be certain of—a point of surety in professional engagements that follow few set patterns and in which we are often on the spot, having to think and feel what it is never possible to prepare for.

This phenomenon—the ingestion of the canon—is endemic in much of psychoanalytic education. However much reading we have done, however lively and clinically structured are the seminars we take part in, the concepts we have been introduced to don't quite marry up in a straightforward way when we start clinical work. The actual experience of being with an individual who is in great distress produces considerable concern that we get it right for that person. The activity of doing psychoanalysis or psychoanalytic therapy throws things at us for which we rarely can be adequately prepared, and thus it is not surprising that we find reassurance in received knowledge.

Received knowledge is critical. We all rely on it. But psychoanalysis is a science in which the properties of what we are studying change over time, over culture, and cannot be applied unthinkingly from one person to another or from one therapeutic dyad to another. Psychoanalysis is an approach to the study of the human being; it is a discipline that studies subjectivity in the process of change and it is an enabling "treatment" for mental distress. The accretion of these various knowledges on the part of the individual practitioner is necessarily slow. How the individual understands what they are learning will, of course, refer to the theories they find useful and the supervisory and clinical relationships they have themselves experienced. Every psychotherapist who works with meaning discovers soon enough that there are few, if any, off-the-shelf interpretations that are of any value when actually working with an individual.

People fit into psychologically derived categories—but not precisely. There are bits that stick out and don't quite match up. Our broadest diagnostic terms are too crude to describe the individual as we meet her or him in their richness and complexity. Nor can an individual predict or fully describe the countertransferential responses and intersubjective experience that mark the therapy. So psychotherapists have to balance what they are learning with what they don't know and with the book knowledge, training, and seminars they have absorbed.

This produces dilemmas. New ideas can be seen as threatening to psychoanalysis. It can take very many attempts to get them taken seriously. The history of psychoanalysis involves splits and the starting of new societies when new trajectories for understanding the human being emerge. In time, new knowledge gets informally adopted or theories that clash sit aside one another and more liberal psychoanalytic societies teach the development of psychoanalytic ideas so that differing theories can be understood contextually. Rarely, however, are new ideas debated and taken up straightforwardly as they might be in another discipline, such as the physics of particles and fields where there is enough confidence to engage with what may at first seem foreign, ridiculous, or heretical.

From both the outside and the inside, the difficulty that psychoanalysis has in discussing new ideas seems perverse. Here is a discipline that can hear what often cannot be heard, that deals in chaotic unformulated thoughts and passionate affects, that encourages the saying of whatever comes into the analysand's mind, and yet is often unable to countenance new ideas that emerge from within its ranks. Part of why it can't do this is because of the special properties of clinical psychoanalysis: the taking on of the emotional distress of the other in a clinical setting and the sense that one has the analysand's life in one's hands. This conjunction—our capacity to be open to whatever comes at us in the clinical situation and the vulnerability we experience in knowing how very much is riding on this therapy for this person—makes an extraordinary demand on us. We require of ourselves that we are emotionally and intellectually alert and yet something goes, and I wonder if what goes isn't our capacity to re-engage with ideas we have come to take so much for granted that we fail to interrogate them.

And so to touch. This is surely a time for us to put our thinking about touch on the agenda. We need to engage the topic in a sufficiently open way so that our discussions about it are useful and open. Psychoanalysis has been with us for well over a century. During this period there have been significant social changes that have impacted on the doctor–patient relationship, rendering it a far different relationship to the one in which touch became considered taboo. There have also been significant changes in society's conception of childhood and parenting. The significance and importance of benign and welcoming touch in development has received much attention in war studies, from biopsychology and from neuro-psychoanalysis. Inside psychoanalytic theory, a widespread exploration of countertransference and the analyst's subjective experience of the therapy have given us a new tool with which to extend our thinking about what occurs in the clinical situation and the pressures the therapist feels within the therapy relationship. The settings in which psychoanalytic work (and its offshoots) occur have extended from private consulting rooms and hospitals to community clinics, medical settings, and GP surgeries, thus providing us with a very large pool of clinical work to draw upon. Then, too, we have significant cross-cultural experience because this very central European discipline has been practised now across Latin America, Western Europe, and in the Anglo-American tradition.

All these developments situate psychoanalysis and psychoanalytic knowledge in a very different place from where it was when the taboos on touch came in. This is not to say that the taboo should be lifted. But it is to say that we need to begin to have a discussion—beyond the scope of this book—that addresses the issue of touch. We need to engender a discipline-wide conversation and research project that would provide the kind of information that would help us formulate questions that need addressing in order for a proper evaluation of the role of touch to be considered.

I don't think this is so difficult. I believe it would be possible to send out anonymous questionnaires to solicit information from practitioners on when and why they touched, why they refrained, when they felt inclined to, how they responded when they were touched, and so on. The need for an anonymous questionnaire arises because, while there is a sense that there is a great deal more thought about touch (and even enacted), embarrassment keeps this out of the general scientific discourse. An anonymous questionnaire is a mechanism for harvesting valuable information that as yet we are unable to discuss openly.

With such a survey in train, it would be possible to disseminate the results and to select examples and instances in which touch has occurred with a view to understanding their impact and import. It would also provide us with a considerable amount of material on the countertransferential impulse (acted upon or not) to touch. Material from such a survey could be extracted and circulated for discussion in seminars. Some discussion has occurred around this, particularly in regard to the emotional pressure that can occur in working with those people who have experienced inappropriate touch in childhood, but while this is extremely useful it is with too limited a population and is essentially anecdotal so that it cannot take on the scrutiny of a more studied question.

The mutative powers of psychoanalysis were first laid at the doors of the interpretation that reached unconscious material. This was what allowed the individual to change. Today I think we believe that what enables people to feel differently inside themselves is the capacity to experience themselves as understood in all their complexity. A complete interpretation situates unconscious processes, the conscious hesitancy and conflicts, the defence structures and the defensive manoeuvres that make those longed-for wishes and desires so very difficult for the individual, within her (present and past) relationships. Interpretation, in other words, is a concept that involves in its very essence the notion of reaching and touching someone emotionally on many levels simultaneously. The cognitive can only provide an "aha" if the emotional timbre of the words reverberates with the feeling states—defensive and desirous—of the individual. Psychoanalysis is affect laden. It disturbs the very emotional deals the individual (and those around her or him) have made with her or himself. This disturbance and the feelings affect it produces is not something we any longer consider a "regression" *per se*. We view it as an accompaniment to change. Psychoanalysis is not the surgical identification of neurosis—and, of course, it never was, although it was sometimes portrayed as such. It is a deeply intersubjective process that alights on various themes, contradictions, and impediments as it unfolds and touches the individuals doing therapy together.

I stress this because affect is physical. So, of course, is thought. There is no such thing as a human being without a body. Descartes's formulation was never tenable. Psychoanalysis has the capacity to think through its own historically derived limitations and to embrace the new scholarship that would defetishize the taboo on discourse about touch. I repeat, we do know that touch occurs, we do know that the desire to touch is elicited in the therapist, we do know that we have a store of clinical experience where touch was privately thought about or enacted. What we need now is serious consideration of the topic so that Spitz's observations, the work of Harlow, and that of Tiffany Field and Ashley Montague, can join together with the work of therapists across the spectrum who use touch and can guide our work in the future.

Many therapists from the body tradition use touch and breathing and the placing of hands in particular places on the body to elicit or unblock feeling. For this kind of practice there is a huge literature that is somewhat outside the scope of what I am suggesting. We on the psychoanalytic wing have much to learn from this. I, for example, am particularly interested in the different meaning(s) a body therapist attaches to a hug at the end of a session as opposed to holding or applying pressure during a session. I am fascinated to learn how a body therapist understands their own bodily countertransferential feelings. I am interested in knowing in what circumstances a body therapist would not touch, and so on. But initially I think psychoanalytic clinicians may need to gather and reflect on our own desire to touch, our fear of touching, our responses when asked to touch, our responses to being touched or wanting to, before we go to the body therapists' literature, which is specific and particular. Through a study of our own countertransference we can comment on our subjective experience in an entirely novel way, and it is to this that I believe we need to turn our attention so that if we do indeed continue with the taboo on touch we know why we do so. We do it mindfully rather than canonically. To manage that would be to strengthen contemporary psychoanalysis.

# Introduction

*Graeme Galton*

Sigmund Freud stopped using the "pressure technique" at some point between 1896 and 1899—we do not know the exact date. Using this technique, he would press lightly on his patient's head while insisting that they remembered forgotten events. He gave up this technique in favour of encouraging free association, then listening and interpreting without touching his patient in any way. Psychoanalysis was born and the use of touch, as a technique reminiscent of hypnosis, was explicitly prohibited (Freud, 1904a). The avoidance of physical contact between the analyst and patient was established as a key component of the classical principle of abstinence.

It is worth remembering just how revolutionary this aspect of psychoanalysis was, representing a fundamental paradigm shift from previous treatments. Out of all medical and therapeutic treatments, psychoanalysis remains one of the very few that uses no physical contact. The history of the treatment of mental illness is dominated by treatments that were very physical, ranging from trepanation (boring holes in the skull) to cold baths and electric shocks. No wonder then that the absence of physical contact became a distinguishing paradigm of psychoanalytic work. Despite occasional questioning from notable figures who included Sándor Ferenczi, Michael Balint, Harold Searles and Donald Winnicott, touch remains virtually non-existent in adult psychoanalytic work; indeed there is almost an unspoken taboo against even discussing it.

None the less, there is evidence to suggest that on rare occasions touch is used carefully and thoughtfully by some psychoanalysts and psychoanalytic psychotherapists, but is kept as a somewhat shameful secret. Such actions may be kept from the scrutiny of supervisors and colleagues because it is feared they would call into question the professional integrity of the psychotherapist concerned. How strange and inappropriate this silence seems in a profession that is founded on the treatment principle that, in the consulting room at least, anything can be spoken of and thought about.

One widely held psychoanalytic viewpoint is that touching a patient serves either to relieve the anxiety of the patient or therapist and does not promote psychic change, or, at worst, leads to sexual relations between therapist and patient. However, I believe there are other possibilities and it seems to me that a subtle shift in emphasis has begun in the debate about touch in the psychoanalytic setting. Michael Balint (1968) and Donald Winnicott (1963) were concerned with physical contact in the context of treating patients who were regressed, with touch occasionally used as a means of containment. John Bowlby (1988) writes that "there are occasions when it would be inhuman not to allow a distressed patient to make some form of physical contact . . ." (p. 154). More recently, the contemporary debate about physical contact has moved beyond containment to also encompass a re-examination of the role of the body in psychotherapy (e.g., Farrell, Chapter Eight; Orbach, 2003a,b).

The origins of this book lie in my own singular experience of physical contact with a patient (Galton, Chapter Six), after which I felt uncertain and rather guilty. I discussed the circumstances at length with colleagues, who offered a variety of thoughts on the rights and wrongs of my clinical judgement. I also recalled the words of one of my supervisors from when I was training as a psychotherapist, who advised us that if we encountered a problem or something new in our work, we now have 100 years of psychoanalytic literature to draw on. We should seek out what has already been written on the issue in question, in the certain knowledge that someone will have written about it in the past. However, when I went looking for references I found that very little had been published on the subject of physical contact in the consulting room. Most of the limited literature was not psychoanalytically-informed and the available literature that was based in psychoanalytic thinking seemed, almost without exception, to be arguing in favour of allowing the use of touch. Interestingly, the few papers on this subject were mostly written by American clinicians. Although they differed in the detail, the majority who had written on this subject had done so out of a conviction that touch in the consulting room could sometimes be helpful for patients. There were occasional exceptions, including one or two writers who offered explanations for why they did not allow physical contact (e.g., Casement, 1982), but there seemed to be a great silent majority whose diverse views were not adequately represented in print. To me, the range of perspectives seemed rather limited and rather one-sided, and was of little help in my own thinking on the subject.

In approaching potential contributors to this volume, I particularly wanted to encompass the widest range of psychoanalytic perspectives and widest range of clinical populations. The clinicians who have contributed to this collection are either psychoanalysts or psychoanalytic psychotherapists, with the addition of a chapter by forensic therapists using psychoanalytic principles (Ramsden, Pryor, Bose, Charles, & Adshead, Chapter Twelve) and a chapter by an analytic body psychotherapist (Totton, Chapter Eleven). Some contributors were initially surprised to be invited to write on the subject of touch, but all have responded with thoughtful and well-argued papers. One of the challenges they faced was the paucity of published literature on the subject. Without a body of directly related previous work upon which to draw, they were entering uncharted waters and deserve special credit for their courageous explorations.

I must mention here that from a few colleagues there was also a negative response to this project. They expressed the view that it was unwise to be associated with this subject because even to talk about touch would be taken as an endorsement of this reckless and dangerous behaviour. One colleague even warned me that this book might damage my reputation. Perhaps this goes some way towards explaining why so little has been written about touch in the psychoanalytic setting. Even Winnicott, who did sometimes use touch with his patients, wrote that he thought it would be unwise to discuss this aspect of his work in print because it could so easily be misunderstood (Kahr, Chapter One).

* * *

In Chapter One, Brett Kahr draws upon his detailed knowledge and understanding of Donald Winnicott's work to ask whether Winnicott's experiments with physical contact were a creative innovation or a chaotic impingement. Kahr identifies a tension in Winnicott's work between his allegiance towards orthodox Freudian psychoanalysis and his attempts to modify treatment by using touch, albeit infrequently, to meet what he perceived as the needs of his more unwell patients.

A. H. Brafman, in Chapter Two, questions the notion that some patients' early developmental deprivations justify or require touch from their analyst. He writes that he has never had a patient who regressed to an emotional position that necessitated any other than the ordinary tools of analytic practice. Brafman suggests that, rather than physical contact meeting the needs of the patient, perhaps it is really the analyst's needs which are being met when he or she touches a patient.

For Chapter Three, the distinguished Jungian analyst Camilla Bosanquet has comprehensively revised and updated for this collection a paper that she first published thirty-six years ago. She argues that a symbolic understanding of tactile communication in psychotherapy allows for the possibility that it can be part of the ongoing analytic process rather than an interference. Bosanquet includes a very moving fragment of a long analysis she began in 1962, working with a depressed and suicidal female patient for whom, at one stage in the treatment, touch became an important element of the analysis.

Chapter Four features Valerie Sinason's pioneering work with children and adults who have suffered extreme experiences of trauma and disability. She suggests that, in some circumstances, touch withheld may be experienced as a re-enactment, in the transference, of the patient's cold, withdrawn mother. She has also found that touch is sometimes useful in alleviating her patient's sense of disgust with themselves.

The distinguished psychoanalyst Pearl King reminds us, in Chapter Five, that cultural context contributes to the meaning of physical contact. She also maintains that, like everything else that occurs in the transference situation, if touch occurs it can usefully be explored and thought about, particularly with adult neurotic patients. She concludes with a moving account of her analysis of a four-year-old boy which was supervised by Winnicott and involved physical contact.

In Chapter Six, I describe an instance of deliberate brief physical contact with a patient in my own clinical practice. I explore in detail some of the issues that I think were relevant to this situation with this patient, a woman who had suffered severe and ongoing sexual, physical and psychological abuse when she was a child and adolescent and whose body still carried serious injuries from these experiences. I also try to assess the effect of this touching on her subsequent psychotherapy.

Nicola Diamond explores the ingrained prejudices regarding touch which have led to its prohibition in psychoanalysis in Chapter Seven, and then asks: what is the nature of touch and what potential has touch as a communicative sense? She presents a multi-disciplinary understanding of touch that brings together ideas from psychoanalysis, attachment theory, developmental psychology, anthropology, linguistics, phenomenology, and neuroscience.

Chapter Eight is contributed by Em Farrell, who draws upon her experience of working with anorexic and bulimic individuals and suggests that more conscious and concrete acknowledgement of the body is needed in psychoanalytic psychotherapy. She suggests that just as the psychotherapist's mind and words are the objects of unconscious phantasy, so, too, is the therapist's body, and she or he may need to be more aware of this and make more use of it in the consulting room.

In Chapter Nine, Maria Emilia Pozzi explores the issue of physical contact in clinical work with babies, young and older children, and adolescents, including those with learning and physical disabilities, autism, psychosis, and developmental delays. She suggests that for these patients physical and psychological hurts, pleasures, and needs are often inseparable, in contrast with adults, where there is usually an adult part that can accept verbalization of the need for physical contact.

The noted psychoanalyst Robert Langs presents, as Chapter Ten, a detailed and uncompromising argument against any physical contact between therapist and patient. He outlines the principles of a new and distinctive paradigm of psychoanalysis: the strong adaptive approach—also known as the communicative approach. Langs argues that the most crucial transactions in psychotherapy involve the management of its conditions—its rules, frames and boundaries—and that departures from these are disruptive and harmful and are a denial-based defence against death anxiety.

Nick Totton, as an analytic body psychotherapist, reminds us in Chapter Eleven that body psychotherapy may or may not involve physical contact between client and therapist, but that touch can function as a bridge between somatic and psychic modes of experience for his patients. He gives us a clear and thoughtful analysis of the use of touch in body psychotherapy and how it connects with, and differs from, mainstream psychoanalytic thinking.

Finally, in Chapter Twleve, Emma Ramsden, Angela Pryor, Sarita Bose, Sharmila Charles, and Gwen Adshead discuss their work as therapists in a secure forensic psychiatric hospital, and consider the complexities of touch when working with patients who have committed serious acts of violence. They also examine the issue of unwanted physical contact—either by patients or by staff—which can carry particular unconscious meaning and significance in this most challenging clinical environment.

* * *

I would like to extend my very warmest thanks to all the talented and thoughtful clinicians who have generously contributed to this volume. I would especially like to thank Susie Orbach, who warmly encouraged me to write on this subject and whose ideas contributed enormously to my thinking. Valerie Sinason has my deepest gratitude for her invaluable support and encouragement as this book took shape. Finally, I owe a special debt to Brett Kahr, who first suggested to me that a collection of essays such as this would be a useful contribution to the body of psychoanalytic literature.

The opinions expressed by the contributors to this volume are their own, and inclusion in this collection does not imply agreement between them. Indeed, it is the wide diversity of views expressed here that makes this collection of essays unique and offers a valuable opportunity to open up debate on this important subject.

# CHAPTER ONE

# Winnicott's experiments with physical contact: creative innovation or chaotic impingement?

*Brett Kahr*

ostile critics of psychoanalysis sometimes assume that
analytical practitioners blindly follow a set of rules of
technique, arbitrarily dictated by Sigmund Freud nearly
one hundred years ago. Although Freud based his recommendations upon his extensive experience with patients from his clinical
practice, it would not be unreasonable to suggest that, in fact,
psychoanalytical technique has not moved much beyond Freud's
essential use of the couch, the free associative method, and the
analysis of transference and resistance. A small band of technical
innovators, however, has attempted to move forward from Freud's
original approach, sometimes to the chagrin of more classically
orientated practitioners. The English paediatrician and psychoanalyst, Dr Donald Woods Winnicott (1896–1971), certainly holds a
prominent position among this group. Winnicott extended the
boundaries of classical psychoanalysis in a number of ways, princi-
pally, through his pioneering work with infants and small children
who did not require full analysis on the couch; and, secondarily, he
expanded the purview of psychoanalytical technique to include the
treatment of psychotic and borderline patients (cf. Kahr, 1996).

In startling contrast to the tenets of classical psychoanalysis, Donald Winnicott even included the use of physical contact in his technical armamentarium, especially in the treatment of very ill patients. Many contemporary practitioners, myself included, would perhaps automatically frown upon such so-called innovations as nothing more than instances of Winnicott's seductiveness, or of his unboundaried nature. Yet, although Winnicott could be both seductive and unboundaried in both his professional activities and in his private life, he also boasted a fine intelligence, and a continuously thoughtful capacity. And though I myself refrain from physical contact with patients in clinical practice, I believe that we owe Winnicott our attention on this matter, and that it might be useful to embark upon an examination of his views on physical contact in more careful detail.

There can be no doubt that Winnicott touched his patients with his hands. We have no idea how extensively he employed physical contact in his psychotherapeutic work, but as far as I can surmise, on the basis of discussions with Dr Winnicott's surviving colleagues and students, he touched his patients infrequently, and only during states of exceptionally severe distress. He subscribed to the idea that physical holding might sometimes be required as a means of providing extra containment for the neediest of his patients. He wrote a few lines of a letter about this controversial technique to his psychoanalytical colleague, Dr Clifford Scott, with reference to a particular patient, noting that,

> In fact it was necessary for me over a long period of time to hold this patient's hands throughout the analysis, this being the equivalent of certifying her and putting her in a padded cell for the analytic hour. In this way she was able to proceed and to express love and hate. If I failed in this physical way then in actual practice I got hit and hurt and this did no good either to me or to the patient. [Winnicott, 1954b, p. 56]

Most psychoanalysts and psychoanalytical psychotherapists would cringe at the thought of any physical contact with a patient, because, as professionals, we appreciate the heightened emotionality of the clinical session, and we recognize that a pat on the shoulder, though usually harmless and innocuous at a social gathering, could in fact be perceived as either an assault or as a seduction during the course of treatment. Both Dr Robert Langs (1973) and Dr David Livingstone Smith (1991) have written about the dangers of physical contact in their germinal works on the importance of boundaries in the psychoanalytical situation. Winnicott (1967a, p. 171) himself certainly realized the contentiousness of physical contact with patients, commenting that, "I have lectured a great deal on the subject of physical contact between patient and therapist. If one writes these things down one gets very easily misunderstood".

As we know, Freud had used the so-called "pressure" technique during the early days of his neurological practice, placing his hands on the heads of his patients in an almost magical attempt to stimulate the flow of free associations by pressing ideas out from the deep unconscious. After a short while, Freud abandoned this laying on of hands as thoroughly unsatisfactory; and thereafter, apart from the occasional handshake at the start or finish of a session, he refrained from further bodily contact in his professional psychoanalytical work. Indeed, one commentator has suggested that Freud eventually sensed the erotic and seductive aspects of his "pressure" technique, whereupon he then embarked on the ultimately successful transition to the classical approach that we employ today (Smith, 1991). In later years, Freud even castigated his colleague Sándor Ferenczi for cuddling and kissing his patients; and any sensible clinician will recognize the dangerousness of Ferenczi's style.

Winnicott appreciated Freud's very classical stance, and for the most part, he adhered to it; but from time to time, Winnicott either initiated a comforting clasp of the hands, or he found himself as the recipient of physical contact from the patient. Dr John Padel (1991), a distinguished member of The British Psychoanalytical Society, has recalled an extraordinary example of a physical interaction between Donald Winnicott and a female analysand. Winnicott had shared this story with Padel and other students at The Institute of Psychoanalysis in London during a teaching seminar from the early 1950s. Apparently, the woman in question had a lithe body, and good acrobatic skills; and one day, during the middle of her analytical session on the couch, she performed a backwards somersault, and thereby deposited herself directly on Winnicott's lap as he sat in the chair nearby. At times, patients do remove themselves from the analytical couch before the session has ended, but to the best of my knowledge, nobody has yet reported such an incomparable occurrence of a woman catapulting off the couch, and on to the body of the clinician.

Needless to say, this event flabbergasted Winnicott considerably, and he presented this story to his startled students, enquiring how they might have reacted in a similar situation. According to Dr Padel, Winnicott responded to this unusual event with exceptional wisdom and sensitivity. He no doubt realized that if he had permitted the woman to remain in his lap, she might have developed a phantasy that all future sessions would be conducted in this position, or she might have become aroused by the proximity to Winnicott's penis, or, he might have become aroused by the contact, and thus experienced an erection. Winnicott knew that this lady would have to leave his lap, yet he also understood her regressive need to be in this position, just like a little child with a parent. In a moment of sheer clinical inspiration, Winnicott gently stood up on his feet, and the woman slid off his lap; but, simultaneously, he placed his hand on her shoulder so that the shift from the chair to the floor would not be too abrupt. Winnicott then maintained his hand on her shoulder and paced up and down the consulting room with her, urging the woman to recall the very last thought that had flashed through her mind before she had performed her somersault. In this way, Winnicott succeeded in preserving his professional psychoanalytical demeanour, and, as Dr Padel has explained, he had thus stopped the most intensively seductive component of the interaction without needing to reject his analysand. Instead, Winnicott had used his hand as a transitional measure, and he speedily returned to the familiar role of analysing the fantasies that stimulate our behaviours.

We can certainly applaud Winnicott for his tact and for his composure during such a difficult and challenging episode. Goodness only knows how anyone else might have dealt with such a singular clinical predicament. Yet, we must also wonder in what way Winnicott himself may have unconsciously stimulated the backwards somersault in the first place. After all, many psychotherapists and counsellors work with challenging patients, but few of these people end up in the clinician's lap without overt permission or seduction. Could it be that on previous occasions, Winnicott had actually held the hand of this acrobatic woman, thus enticing her to do something more dramatic at a later time? We cannot answer this question with any degree of certainty as we simply do not have access to any other details from the treatment.

The autobiographical report written by Winnicott's analysand Margaret Little (1985), can perhaps provide important insights about Winnicott's use of the hand-holding technique. Dr Little, a psychoanalyst in her own right who had undergone many years of treatment with Donald Winnicott, became quite regressed at various points during her analysis, and on such occasions, both parties would clasp one another's hands. At one point during the midst of the analysis, Winnicott had announced the dates of his forthcoming summer holiday. He then urged Dr Little to enter a psychiatric hospital during this time because he feared that she might commit suicide during his absence. Little flew into a rage at the prospect of being abandoned by her psychoanalyst for the summer, and, as far as she can recollect, she began to hit out at Winnicott. In an attempt to protect both himself and his patient, Winnicott "Caught my wrists and held me, and was not hurt" (Little, 1985, p. 32). One can certainly appreciate the necessity of such touching, because both the psychotherapist and the patient must remain physically unharmed in order for the psychoanalytical treatment to continue. But on other occasions, Winnicott held Margaret Little for somewhat different reasons, in the absence of any physical attack.

In one particular instance, Little (1985, p. 20) grabbed Winnicott's hands and "clung tightly" in the middle of a spasm of terror. According to her account, the ability to maintain contact with Winnicott's body permitted Little to survive the awful spasm, and to recover from it: "Those spasms never came again, and only rarely that degree of fear" (Little, 1985, p. 20). But at other times, Winnicott himself would initiate the hand-holding, but only during periods of great emotional turmoil for his patient. Dr Little (1985, p. 21) recalled: "Literally, through many long hours he held my two hands clasped between his, almost like an umbilical cord, while I lay, often hidden beneath the blanket, silent, inert, withdrawn, in panic, rage or tears, asleep and sometimes dreaming."

One can readily appreciate the possible curative aspects of these various situations: clasping the shoulder of an acrobat who jumped into his lap, fending off the punches of an angry and hurt woman, and providing gentle containment of extreme anguish. But Winnicott also performed another variety of physical touch with Margaret Little. He used a thermometer to take her temperature, and he undertook other medical investigations as well. At this juncture, we must quote Dr. Little's own words exactly: "He was always concerned for my physical state; he kept stethoscope, sphygmomanometer and clinical thermometer handy, and used them" (Little, 1985, p. 27). We do not know how often Winnicott related to Margaret Little in such an overtly medical way, but regardless, we have now accumulated enough data to suggest that Winnicott touched his patients, beyond the traditional handshake at the time of the first consultation. As we know, such medical contact defies the boundaries of all good principles of psychotherapeutic practice. There can be absolutely no suggestion that Winnicott ever committed a genitally abusive act with a patient. Our data provide not the slightest inkling of such an impropriety; besides, a sexual assault would have been completely uncharacteristic of Winnicott, a man who tended to internalize hostile feelings rather than externalize them in an assaultative manner (Kahr, 1996). But in spite of the episodic and perhaps unerotic nature of Winnicott's touches, we must begin to evaluate the effects of such behaviour.

All psychoanalytically orientated psychotherapists regard physical contact between the clinician and the patient with such consternation that most textbooks do not even mention this prohibition explicitly. One simply does not touch one's patients, and the subject need be mentioned no further. Exceptionally, the thoughtful American psychoanalyst, Dr Robert Langs (1973), has devoted an entire section of his first superbly detailed textbook on the technique of psychoanalytical psychotherapy to the topic of "Not touching the patient". Dr Langs (1973, p. 200) has stated firmly and clearly that, "touching is contraindicated and anti-therapeutic" because it gratifies omnipotent phantasies of controlling the psychotherapist, and it prevents the development of insight. Langs does acknowledge that a handshake at the first assessment interview, or at the start of a new year of treatment can be offered, and that touching would also be appropriate in a medical emergency. In this regard, Langs has cited the case of a woman who told her analyst that her foot had fallen asleep, and that she had begun to topple over while standing in the consulting room. The psychoanalyst, of course, used his arm to support the patient, thus breaking her fall. In all such emergencies, though, one must always analyse the meaning and the fantasies surrounding the physical contact afterwards.

Incidentally, a number of years ago, I had the opportunity to discuss this clinical vignette with Langs nearly twenty years after he first wrote about it (personal communication, 15th May 1992). He told me that nowadays he would not have recommended that an analyst offer his or her arm to a patient in such circumstances, as his extensive clinical experience has led him to realize that the patient would have felt great unconscious hostility about any bodily contact.

Some psychoanalysts adopt an even more boundaried approach than Robert Langs, himself an extremely classical practitioner. I have met some psychotherapists who would not shake hands at the start of a new year of treatment, or even at the end of a lengthy five-times weekly analysis, unless the patient specifically wished to do so. I also know of one case concerning an analyst who refused to shake the patient's hand at the conclusion of a very lengthy, full analysis, even though the patient urged the analyst to do so. The psychoanalyst in question clung to the prohibition against physical contact, and wanted to preserve the "analytical" nature of the relationship in case the patient should ever wish to return for more treatment at some point in the future.

I realize that certain readers from the humanistic or behavioural schools of counselling might regard these handshaking details with some contempt. After all, virtually everybody shakes hands in the outside world, so why should this pose a problem? In brief, Freudian practitioners deliberate over these small points with such care because we realize that any physical interaction between two people can so easily trigger unconscious memories of earlier physical interactions, especially those of a provocative or abusive nature. As our understanding of the widespread occurrence of child sexual abuse improves, ranging from actual rape to the seductive bathing of the infant's genitalia, we know that even simple touching can often exert a re-traumatizing effect on the patient (cf. Smith, 1991).

Patrick Casement (1982), a British psychoanalyst who works within a broad Winnicottian tradition, has written an important paper about this subject, and it has already become something of a classic, widely quoted, and much discussed. Mr Casement's essay, entitled "Some pressures on the analyst for physical contact during the re-living of an early trauma", concerns a female analysand of some thirty-odd years of age, who insisted that she be permitted to hold Casement's hand as she worked through the memory of an infantile trauma. At the age of eleven months, this woman pulled a container of boiling water on to herself; and, as a consequence, she had to undergo an operation on her skin six months later. The patient's mother held her hand during the operation, performed under a local anaesthetic; yet the mother fainted, and the little girl remembered the awful feeling of her mother's hand slipping away. In view of this disturbing experience, one can certainly understand why the patient would want to hold on to the hand of her analyst.

This particular patient even threatened to quit the analytical treatment if Casement did not comply with her request for his hand, and as the tension mounted, Casement became so worried that he thought this woman might actually end up in a psychiatric hospital. Admirably, Patrick Casement considered the demand for physical contact with great seriousness. He chose not to follow analytical precepts dogmatically, but, instead, he wrote that, "the possibility of physical contact was approached as an open issue" (Casement, 1982, p. 279). Although he felt very tempted to help his analysand through the trauma by lending a helping hand—quite literally—after careful reflection, he eventually decided to refrain from any physical contact.

One might be inclined to believe that Casement should have extended his hand, symbolically replacing that of the mother whose hand disappeared as she fainted during the critical operation. But Casement must have known that even if he did give her a hand, he would have needed to withdraw it at the end of the fifty-minute session. Moreover, the patient presented a dream image in which a child reached out to touch a motionless figure whom she thought to be Mr Casement; yet as she did so, this person "crumbled and collapsed" (Casement, 1982, p. 281). Unconsciously, she thus succeeded in communicating to her analyst that though she craved physical contact, she also feared that her neediness would cause Casement to wither, thus repeating the behaviour of the fainting mother who really did crumble. Through the analysis of this dream fragment, both parties discovered that Casement could be more therapeutic by being different from the woman's mother, hence preventing the trauma from reoccurring; therefore, no physical exchange transpired between the psychoanalyst and the patient.

Returning to Winnicott, let us consider whether he handled his encounter with Margaret Little as well as he might have done. In order to answer this question, we must consider the important work of David Livingstone Smith (1991), the author of an excellent book, *Hidden Conversations: An Introduction to Communicative Psychoanalysis*, who has written perceptively on the importance of maintaining classical boundaries in the clinical setting. Smith has discovered that though patients may sometimes praise their psychotherapists for hand-holding and for other seemingly nurturant gestures, as Margaret Little has done, the unconscious, encoded stories that patients then tell invariably reveal a sense of betrayal and seduction. For example, Smith (1989) has published a case related to him by Dr Robert Langs. In this clinical vignette, a woman patient dropped her sweater on the floor of the consulting room, and her psychotherapist, a man, picked up the garment and handed it to her. Although the patient appeared grateful to her psychotherapist for having retrieved her garment, she actually arrived late for her next appointment after having dreamed that her brother had touched her breast. Of course, the sweater covers the breast area of a woman's body, and it seems evident that she felt molested by her male psychotherapist for having touched such an intimate article of her clothing.

Interestingly, when we consider Margaret Little's account, we learn of her great admiration for Winnicott, and of the many ways in which he had saved her life. But, in addition to the praise, we also hear quite a lot about Winnicott's numerous illnesses; and though he did suffer from many physical complaints during the course of Little's analysis, one wonders whether she also perceived Winnicott as ill in other ways. For instance, after Little has discussed Winnicott's heart attack, she then quickly begins to recount the occasion when Winnicott referred to her own mother as an ill and unreliable person. According to Dr Little, Winnicott had said: "Your mother is unpredictable, chaotic, and she organizes chaos around her", and further, that, "She's like a Jack-in-a-box, all over the place" (Little, 1985, p. 24). David Smith has suggested to me (personal communication, 3 December 1991) that though this vibrant image of the undependable Jack-in-a-box certainly describes Little's mother quite well, it also provides an accurate depiction of Dr Winnicott during the analysis. After all, though Little has told us about Winnicott's classical interpretations and his professional abilities, we have also discovered that he took her temperature, and her blood pressure, and even listened to the sound of her chest; he visited her at home; he extended the length of her sessions; he sent her postcards from his holidays; he offered her biscuits and coffee; he presented her with a handkerchief; he discussed his personal life with her; he spoke to her at the weekend; he held her hands; he took charge of her car keys on one occasion; he even permitted her to rest in his house after her sessions had ended; and he discussed her case with one of Little's personal friends, and so forth. Winnicott even helped Little to put on her coat at the end of the session, a further opportunity for close physical proximity between the two people (Anderson, 1981).

Although these breaches of the classical boundaries may have provided Margaret Little with considerable gratification, they also recapitulated the Jack-in-a-box style of mothering that Little had experienced in girlhood to a certain extent. By the way, it cannot be accidental that the French psychoanalyst Simone Decobert (1984, p. xi) had referred to Winnicott, quite independently, as "A jack-in-the-box", after having met him at a conference in Copenhagen.

One could readily protest that because of Little's regressions, and because of her marked infantile state, she needed Winnicott to abandon his traditional, classical approach, and thus provide some of the basic maternal care that she had sorely lacked. A large literature has begun to emerge on this very stimulating topic, considering what changes, if any, must be made to work with more distressed patients (cf. Eissler, 1953). Dr Elizabeth Moberly (1985), a shrewd psychoanalytical psychologist, has argued that it does not suffice to interpret verbally to regressed patients that they suffer from unfulfilled dependency needs; instead, one must offer a corrective emotional experience by gratifying some of those needs in a reasonable way. And Winnicott's talented colleague, Mrs Barbara Dockar-Drysdale (1974, p. 4), has introduced us to the phrase "the provision of primary experience" in her work with psychotic children. If a youngster has suffered extremes of deprivation, one does not simply interpret; rather, one provides this primary experience in other words, some basic caretaking that the troubled individual has never received. A small girl called Susan, one of Mrs Dockar-Drysdale's psychotic patients, called out for a fried egg and for some hot chocolate. Dockar-Drysdale could have rendered a verbal interpretation to the child that the request for eggs and chocolate represented a deep, unconscious wish for breasts and for breast milk, but she preferred to satisfy Susan's hunger in a very concrete way. As Barbara Dockar-Drysdale (1974, p. 4) noted, "I knew the egg was a breast, but I did not feel that interpretation would be appropriate". After roughly a year of this primary maternal provision, Susan no longer needed real, concrete food in her treatment; she could now be content with more traditional methods of treatment. Of course, Susan undertook her healing in the context of a residential setting, which encourages regression, and so the bodily gratification must be understood in this context.

By contrast, the more orthodox school of psychoanalysis would not rely on physical contact in any way, nor encourage the fulfilment of any bodily wishes beyond the provision of a safe and comfortable treatment room. As Hanna Segal (1979, p. 80) has stated, without equivocation, "The appropriate expression of love by the analyst is understanding." In fact, though Winnicott would gratify physical needs by offering biscuits and coffee, he also knew that an orthodox session with continual good listening could be just as nourishing, if not more so. In a footnote to one of his essays, Winnicott (1960, p. 591, fn. 1) commented: "A patient said to me: 'A good analytic hour in which the right interpretation is given at the right time is a good feed'". Obviously, this debate can become quite complex, and it could readily exceed the purview of this essay (cf. Winnicott, 1954a). Yet, once again, we encounter a full-blooded tension in Winnicott's work between his allegiance towards orthodox Freudian psychoanalysis and his attempts to modify the treatment to suit what he perceived as the needs of the more unwell patients.

In 1986, an American woman called Evelyn Walker published an autobiography, chillingly entitled A Killing Cure, which describes the ways in which her analyst, then a fully accredited member of the American Psychoanalytic Association, enticed her to have sexual intercourse on the analytical couch, during her session time (Walker & Young, 1986). Winnicott certainly never abused his professional position in such a dramatic and horrific manner, but he did break away from the advice and guidelines of his teachers and his colleagues by holding hands with patients in a gentle manner, at a time when other clinicians treated extremely regressed patients quite successfully without any physical contact (e.g., Rosenfeld, 1947, 1949, 1950, 1952; Segal, 1950, 1956). Personally, I would not recommend hand-holding in work with regressed patients, as I know that one can "hold" a patient in distress with one's voice, or with one's eyes, or with the right verbal intervention. I believe that colleagues who have held the hands of their patients have at times stunted the sexual development of these individuals by fostering unrealistic phantasies of marrying the psychotherapist. Still, this aspect of Winnicott's technique will remain a highly controversial point for some time to come, especially outside of psychoanalytical circles.

In respect of the use of the stethoscope, or thermometer, or sphygmomanometer (blood pressure cuff) in the treatment of Dr Little, I find this all very shocking, to say the least, because the application of such diagnostic tools requires very intimate bodily contact indeed. Such medical procedures consist of the insertion of a long, thin rod into the mouth, the placing of a hard, metallic object to the bare chest, and the pumping of pressure on the arm after having rolled away the sleeve of a blouse or shirt. An American psychoanalyst called Dr Samuel Lipton (1977) once encouraged a febrile analysand to put his thermometer in her mouth during the course of a session, ostensibly for medical reasons. The analysand, a lawyer by profession, refused to do so, although she did, in fact, have a raised temperature at the time. She returned for her next analytical session, and she began to tell a story about one of her own legal cases, expressing chagrin about one customer in particular, fearing that she had "betrayed her client" (Lipton, 1977, p. 469), indicating perhaps that she had experienced Dr Lipton's offered thermometer as some kind sexually abusive betrayal.

Extraordinarily, Winnicott not only used medical instruments with Margaret Little, herself an experienced doctor and former general practitioner, but, at times, he also encouraged her to visit her personal physician or even a specialist medical consultant. So, sometimes he took her temperature, and at other times, he sent her to somebody else for this purpose. But in fact, most astoundingly, after many years of medical training, and then no fewer than eleven years of general practice, Dr Little could easily have taken her own temperature! In this way, Winnicott encouraged regression by stripping Margaret Little of her considerable medical skills.

Finally, as Smith has reminded me (personal communication, 7 January 1992), Margaret Little had approached Winnicott for classical psychoanalysis, and not for hand-holding as such. And as Little had already become qualified as a psychoanalyst herself, she knew exactly what the request for analysis should entail. Though Dr Little did improve dramatically in her treatment with Winnicott, one wonders whether the psychoanalysis could have worked even more effectively without the holding of hands and the many other infringements of basic boundaries. Smith has even suggested (personal communication, 7 January 1992) that Winnicott's penchant for physical contact may have stemmed more from the frustrated parental tendencies of a childless old man than from the demands of the patients themselves.

In contrast to the basic viewpoints of classical psychoanalysis, and the modern revision known as communicative psychoanalysis, Dr Donald Winnicott dared to engage in technical experimentation by touching his highly disturbed patients in small ways, on a small number of occasions. Do we castigate the childless Winnicott for his wish to transform his patients into honorary sons and daughters who could have provided him with a modicum of physical contact, or do we attempt to learn something from his brave work with the sorts of patients that most practitioners would refuse to treat from the outset?

On one occasion, I had to use a very small degree of physical contact to restrain a chronically self-injurious, handicapped, psychotic patient from inflicting further neurological damage upon herself. The patient entered the consulting room on one occasion, and proceeded to smash her head repeatedly against the wall. After several rapid attempts at interpretation and subsequently at verbal injunction, the patient still persisted, and so I had to remove myself from my chair, grab the patient by the shoulders, and move her away from the wall, stating, "I will not permit you to harm yourself in this way during your session. I know you want to show me how much your head hurts, and how angry you are, but we must try to talk about it." Whatever the antecedents of this particular bout of head-banging, the patient might have sustained a cerebral haemorrhage had I not used my hands to pull her shoulders away from the wall.

I can neither endorse nor condemn Winnicott's experimentation with physical contact, particularly as he engaged in this practice at a relatively early stage in the history of psychoanalytical practice when practitioners possessed only a very rudimentary knowledge of the framework of treatment. I offer this evidence primarily as a stimulus to further discussion and research.

# CHAPTER TWO

# Touching and affective closeness

*A. H. Brafman*

I came to England to pursue my analytic training and my psychoanalytic life has unfolded in this country. My analyst, supervisors, and lecturers were all unanimous in teaching that analysis was a process based on words. Of course, as the years went by, we took on board the relevance of non-verbal material, of the personality and style of the analyst, the importance of a diagnostic assessment of the patient's pathology, the elements that presumably differentiated between psychotherapy and "proper" analysis. Needless to say, opinions varied and each of us gradually developed his own style of working with patients. However, curiously enough, touching the patient was usually considered one of the things that "only Dr Winnicott" did with his patients. Touching was one of the unusual things that he provided to those patients who had "regressed to dependence" and these accounts were treated with puzzlement and an implicit sense of condemnation. I am sure that it was the enormous respect and admiration that Winnicott commanded in the British Psychoanalytical Society that precluded overt criticism of his approach to these particular patients. Not many other analysts came forward to inform the world that they treated similar patients or resorted to such technical parameters.

Margaret Little (1985) proved the exception, but then she had been analysed by Winnicott and this was seen as confirmation that touching constituted a technique that characterized the analyst's therapeutic preferences, rather than being exclusively part of a patient's conscious or unconscious needs.

Michael Balint (1968) wrote of touching the patient in *The Basic Fault*, but, as far as I know, this was treated in the same way as Winnicott's procedures: highly idiosyncratic views and definitely not parameters to be adopted by all analysts.

Jonathan Pedder (1976) and Patrick Casement (1982) published papers discussing the issue of touching the patient, but their papers did not lead to many other analysts of the British Psychoanalytical Society writing about this topic. I believe it is fair to say that the general ethos of the British psychoanalytic scene still considers touching the patient as wrong or, at least, dangerous. Apparently, this is not the case in other analytic societies, although not many papers have been published on this issue.

*Psychoanalytic Inquiry* (2000) published an issue entitled "On touch in the psychoanalytic situation" in which Patrick Casement's (1982) paper, "Some pressures on the analyst for physical contact during the reliving of an early trauma", was taken as the focus for discussion by a number of distinguished analysts. There was general agreement that this was a most important paper and each author praised Casement's work. However, several of the papers made it clear that they saw this as a not-too-convincing exposition, clearly written by an orthodox Freudian British psychoanalyst, who appeared defensive and apologetic over his dealing with the patient's wish to hold his hand. The contributors were analysts who had published articles and books advocating the importance of feeling free to touch the patient, all criticizing what they saw as a prejudiced adoption of Freud's rule of abstinence. Contrary to this supposedly Freudian condemnation of touching, they argued that some patients have special needs for physical contact and, provided care was taken to respect the precepts of professional ethics, they saw no reason not to satisfy these needs.

To someone such as myself, coming from a Latin culture (Brazil), it is quite amusing to read discussions that include handshaking as an example of touching the patient. This brought back memories of my first analytic sessions in London, when I shook hands with my analyst and took off my jacket and shoes before lying down on the couch. After some interpretations about the unconscious, transferential meaning of such behaviour, I got the message and adopted proper behaviour best suited to a patient undergoing analysis in Britain: shoes on (so that was the reason for the mat at the end of the couch!), jacket on and no handshakes. Hardly work facilitating insight into the unconscious! But, justice to my analyst, it was her room and we were no longer in my home country. However, I remain unconvinced that I was expressing any particular unconscious need.

I would like to mention some experiences that have influenced my views on the issue of touching.

Many years ago, I saw a man in his mid-thirties for a consultation. We discussed his problems, I agreed that he would benefit from having analysis or psychotherapy and I recommended that he should have at least two or three sessions per week. He came to see me for another two meetings, but he then sent me a letter, informing me that he did not intend to come for further sessions. He told me that he was seeking an analyst who would give him that precise kind of analysis that Winnicott had given Harry Guntrip and some other patients. He was convinced that he had experienced early traumas and now wanted an analyst who would help him to regress to that period of his life. He believed he would need more than just words from his analyst and wanted to see someone who would not hesitate to offer him emotional and physical holding if this became necessary to help him reach back to those early experiences and overcome his present difficulties. As he had concluded that I was not that type of analyst, he thanked me for my efforts but he now wished to seek a more suitable analyst. He was correct in his assessment: I did not believe his complaints suggested any early traumatic experiences.

During our analytic training, we had the privilege of having clinical seminars with Dr Lois Munro, an exceptionally gifted analyst, who is hardly remembered these days. She was in charge of the Clinical Services of the London Clinic of Psycho-Analysis and very active in teaching activities. One evening, when discussing the relationship between patient and analyst, she told us the story of a student analyst who reported in supervision that he had agreed to a female patient performing fellatio on him. We were all duly horrified and there was unanimous outrage at such a practice. Apparently, the student argued that the patient had been experiencing enormous anxiety and gradually came to put into words her conviction that only an intimate physical exchange would soothe her panic. Dr Munro did consider that the patient's psychopathology had some relevance in giving rise to this occurrence, but she gave much more importance to the analyst's neglect of the responsibilities of his position. Obviously, fellatio can hardly be seen as an example of the kind of touching the patient that is under discussion, but this episode still depicts an analyst believing that using his body was more effective than his words, under the conviction that this is what would meet his patient's needs.

Over the years, I have had patients who expressed a wish for physical contact and I have also supervised students whose patients sought such close physical proximity. In one case, a young female patient wormed herself over her analyst's chair to lay her head on the analyst's lap. Another patient many times came very close to me and occasionally touched me on the arm or the leg; this particular female patient would always claim that having physical, if possible sexual, contact with me was her idea of bliss. A colleague working in an in-patient unit told me of a young woman he saw in individual therapy. One day, as she stood up to leave the room, obviously in great pain and anguish, she came closer to him and embraced him. He was taken aback, but felt he could not step back or push her away. But just as he fumbled in his embarrassment at the physical closeness, he noticed he had an erection. Neither at that moment nor subsequently did he attribute this unexpected erection to the patient's psychopathology: he had no doubt that it was linked to the fact of this particular young woman being very attractive. Subsequent experience has confirmed, time and time again, that young, good-looking women invariably move male professionals to respond to them in a dramatically different way to their ordinary manner with patients who are not so attractive. Indeed, this can happen in any sphere of life, but it is particularly dangerous for analysts to ignore their feelings of attraction or repulsion towards a patient: it is a serious mistake to write these off on the basis of attributing them exclusively to countertransference.

Rodman's (2003) biography of Winnicott recounts the case of Corky, a woman who had developed the type of regression that

Winnicott judged justified a number of departures from ordinary analytic technique. The patient took several overdoses and when she could not attend for her sessions Winnicott would see her at her home, often taking his secretary with him, so that she could do the patient's shopping and attend to other domestic chores. When Winnicott was unable to continue her analysis, Masud Khan took over her treatment and, apparently, developed a sexual relationship with her. No doubt, this says something about Khan's attitude to his patients, but the patient's compliance makes me wonder whether her multiple physical demands when seeing Winnicott might also point to a similar capacity to sense her object's needs and expectations, which she could then satisfy. In other words, how can we, as outsiders, ever establish whose needs are being met in such complex and private interactions?

Let us assume there is a point where the patient expresses, verbally or in gestures, the need or the wish to hold the analyst's hand. There are only two possible alternatives: either the analyst does hold the patient's hand or, which is the same, indicates his willingness to do this, or else he uses words to indicate his interpretation of the patient's verbal or non-verbal communication. Whether this becomes an isolated incident or the beginning of a pattern, only further developments will reveal. Whether the patient expresses some deep, early, physical longing or, alternatively, there are sexual elements in this move, again, only further developments will reveal.

My thinking in this matter is very influenced by my views on the issue of physical violence. Whatever the patient's age, at the point where the analyst is attacked, his reaction is fundamental in establishing what is to follow. This has been my experience over children's physical violence, in ongoing analysis or in their ordinary, daily, family life. The first time a child moves a limb in such a way that pain is inflicted on a parent or sibling it is possible that this results from frustration and hostility. But it is equally possible that this is still some spontaneous, accidental movement quite devoid of such emotions. However, the parent's response to this gesture is bound to be experienced by the child as a pointer to the link between that movement and certain affects and impulses; and this may become the beginning of a pattern of behaviour. As a matter of fact, this combination of action and reaction is what characterizes any interaction between two people. If the encounter continues, these behavioural expressions quickly become the expected response that influences each party's contribution to the interaction.

Two important points have to be made in the context of the analytic encounter. One, each patient has his own conscious and unconscious needs, and two, each analyst has (or should have) a clear notion of how he defines his therapeutic role. It is conceivable that the issue of touching might take us to that classical question raised by the behaviour of drunk people: is their behaviour caused by the drink or is it that the drink brought to the surface behaviour that had lain dormant? In my own personal case, I have long been aware of a conscious and unconscious compulsion to help others, but I have also learnt that this need has never taken me to the position of creating or fostering a situation of dependence on me. This, I believe, may well be the reason why I have never managed to keep in treatment patients who wish to remain in analysis forever. Looking back over my many years of analytic practice, I have to admit that I never had a patient who regressed to an emotional position that necessitated any other than the ordinary tools of analytic practice. Is this a case of blindness? Or is it perhaps a professional limitation? I prefer to think that this follows from my understanding of my professional self and I can only hope that I have not failed any of my patients because of this.

Regarding the patient's needs, ideally, we should have access to a laboratory where we could start one patient in simultaneous analysis with two different analysts. If this patient were to plunge into a deep regression, would he come to voice a wish for physical contact with both analysts? And, if so, would both analysts respond in the same way? And what difference would each response make in therapeutic and prognostic terms? The possibility that this hypothetical regressed patient might express a wish to be touched only to one of the two analysts is, clearly, quite disturbing.

To a large extent, the controversy over touching the patient or not has been influenced by Freud's recommendation of the rule of abstinence. Many of the authors who discuss this point emphasize the contradiction with Freud's earlier putting his hand on the patient's forehead. Freud's journey from this technique imported from hypnotism to what became the talking cure may, I believe, parallel his views on having the patient lying down on the couch. But Freud made it explicit that this position was chosen to cater for his dislike of having the patient staring at him during the session, i.e., a choice made for the sake of the analyst's comfort. As is well known, over the decades lying on the couch has become a dogma, and any number of justifications are put forward to implement this rule. I have, in fact, taught students and explained to patients that this position enables the patient to concentrate on his own thoughts and feelings, without the interference of various perceptions of the analyst's movements. Is this the full, honest answer? As the years went by, I came not to be bothered by the patient's lying on the couch or sitting on the chair opposite me, and each patient made his own choice. I believe a similar pattern has occurred over many other issues where patient and analyst are involved: for whose sake is a particular parameter adopted or denied?

My main objection to the arguments aiming at having touching as a regular technical parameter is the emphatic claim that this responds to a patient's needs. When touching is undertaken as the therapist's concept of the appropriate technical step, then I respect his setting out to use physical contact with all or most of his patients: this is his own, private, personal view of his therapeutic tools. Bio-energetics is now quite a widespread technique that adopts this principle of physical touching as a basic parameter. As happens with every single technique put to the public, there will always be people in pain who will believe this is the help they need, while others will shun that practitioner. However, this is not the same as finding arguments in the patient's psychopathology to justify the adoption of touching as an alternative to talking, in order to bring fulfilment to "the patient's needs". I would assume that if a diagnosis is made that the patient will benefit from touching, this should be implemented without the patient having to ask for it. We also find patients who claim to *need* more time than the fifty minutes we allot them: will our colleagues who respond to the patient's need to be touched also grant the patient the time span they ask for? We have patients who desperately beg to have a session on a Sunday morning: how to respond to this need? And the patient who painfully longs to be granted a long break from analysis: do we accept this? Another example, that in the present day will appear absurd: when I trained in the 1960s, many analysts smoked and allowed their patients to smoke. I remember discussions about the analyst being or not being responsible for supplying ashtrays and Kleenex tissues. Presumably, it was universally accepted that smoking was a need that had to be gratified: so, are analysts now prepared to allow patients to smoke during their sessions? The challenge, clearly, lies in the assessment of the unconscious meaning of these wishes, requests, demands. The acceptance of touching is justified by its stemming from early privations—so, conceivably, smoking might be seen as the result of early oral frustrations: do we then allow the patient to smoke?

*Insight*, a publication of the International Psychoanalytical Association (2003), printed a survey of the views of seven analysts on the issue of "telephone analysis". I found this discussion quite fascinating. The present trend of spreading analytic knowledge to students who live far away from training centres has led to some most unusual arrangements. I had heard of supervision sessions and group seminars being conducted on special communication equipment, under the justification of the geographical distance between the places of residence of trainees and the senior analysts involved. But I had never considered telephone conversations with patients as a major issue. I discovered now that some analysts did agree to conduct analytic sessions over the phone (how did they charge for these, I wondered). I am mentioning this survey because even though the patient's wishes are mentioned, considered, and agreed to, I found no reference to early or primitive needs. Analysts seemed to accept that work commitments of their patients might make it impossible for them to attend their consulting rooms and were prepared to embark on whatever arrangement allowed the patient to continue his work with the analyst. I think telephone analysis contains a parallel to the question of touching the patient. In both cases, a patient's wish leads to the analyst's acquiescence, but one is justified by the practicalities of modern living and the other is explained by the primitiveness of the patient's needs. Clearly, not much intellectual ingenuity would be required to postulate "early" anxieties and impulses determining the request for regular telephone contact, and yet these are not considered necessary before agreeing to the patient's request.

A very important point of our present discussion is what will lead the analyst to consider that a patient's wish represents an early, primitive, developmental need that was not fulfilled during the patient's infancy or, instead, a statement that what the analyst normally offers is not sufficient. At the time when Freud, Balint and even the early Winnicott were writing about regressed patients, the analyst saw himself as a professional trying to help his patient. Gradually, a change occurred and many analysts were no longer "the mother in the transference", but gradually came to see themselves as "the mother" who now tried to put right the failures of the patient's real mother. This change took place with the increasing prevalence of the teaching that the analysis of the transference was the main tool of analytic work and, furthermore, that early conflicts had primary significance in the patient's material. Not surprisingly, many or most of the patient's wishes were now seen to stem from early developmental deprivations.

I believe that this is the reason why several authors have taken up the patient's need for physical contact as representing a *reliquat* of their earliest experiences. Arguments have been published emphasizing the extent to which the contact between the baby's skin and the mother's skin is a vital step in the organization of the baby's awareness of his body, his body self. Susie Orbach (2003a,b) emphasizes this point quite forcefully in her arguments to justify, if not to prescribe, the physical contact between patient and therapist. But oral experiences are also considered most important in the infant's growing awareness of the other: so, how should we respond to a patient's wish for oral contact with the analyst's body? Research has now shown that the foetus is influenced by the mother's heartbeats: if the patient wants to rest his/her head on our chest, should we oblige?

I have another difficulty with the definition of "trauma". Casement (1982) emphasizes his patient's traumatic experience: seriously scalded when eleven months old and submitted to surgery at seventeen months of age. During this intervention the patient was holding her mother's hand until the mother fainted. Casement's paper discusses events as "she was reliving this experience". Presumably, Casement is following Balint's and Winnicott's concept of regression to early stages of development. Some of the colleagues who discuss Casement's paper in the issue of *Psychoanalytic Inquiry* (2000) mentioned above, argue that at this point in time we must adopt an interactive, relational, interpersonal view of the analytic encounter, i.e., in what way had Casement contributed to bring the patient to that situation? Clearly, this is an argument that will not allow for a compromise solution. Each analyst's interpretation of his patient is entirely dependent on his own preconceptions. Personally, whenever I heard stories of patients being helped to regress, for example, to the point of the primal scream, I could only wonder about the therapist's powers of persuasion. I have not been convinced, so far, that we retain retrievable true memory traces of those earliest experiences. In other words, I do not know when exactly each individual manages to register his life experiences in a way that these memory traces are available for future years and decades. Perhaps unscientifically, if not cynically, I am one of those who believe that we are forever rewriting our history. In the case of Casement's patient, I would assume that she was not expressing her memory of the events surrounding the burns and the surgery, but rather trying to make sense of her mother's account of those events. I do know that many children feel puzzled when informed of events in their own life that they cannot recall. Depending on their age when told of such happenings, these accounts can be experienced as quite traumatic. On the basis of this assumption, the issue then would be not so much holding hands but rather helping the patient to understand the feelings underlying her mother's words and what feelings these words had brought out in her at whatever the age she was when she first heard them.

I would like to relate two further stories. In a clinical seminar during our analytic training, Michael Balint asked each student how we started and finished our sessions. We all saw our patients in the main building of the Institute of Psycho-Analysis and this meant that all our patients were met at the same waiting room and then taken to each student's assigned room, which was on one of two floors. The result of this exercise was rather surprising. We were twelve students but it turned out that we had not a single example of two of us doing the same thing! Some preceded the patient on the route from waiting room to consulting room, others invited the patient to go first; some shook hands with the patient in the waiting-room, while others barely nodded their head towards the patient while standing at the door. We had a variety of formulae whereby each of us indicated that it was time to finish the session. Some of us would stand up and allow the patient to leave the room, while others opened the door to let the patient out. The only example that caused general surprise was to learn that one of us left the analytic room first, letting the patient organize his/her things and find his/her way out. Needless to say, none of this would ever be known if it had not suddenly become the focus of a discussion. It would be quite fascinating to discover how each of our patients interpreted our behaviour! These rituals seem quite trivial, but this seminar remained a dramatic example that what happens between patient and analyst is only, exclusively, known by the two of them. We can take it for granted that not always will each of them interpret events in the same manner as each other. If only words are questioned, it can be quite difficult to agree on what they meant, but when non-verbal communications are considered, the complications are infinitely worse.

Another interesting example, that I place in the same category, is that of a very eminent analyst who wrote extensively about the analysis of seriously ill patients. His papers demanded the strictest adherence to orthodox boundaries. He argued that analysis was a verbal process and that primary attention had to be given to the analysis of the transference. I met a colleague who consulted this analyst for supervision of an extremely difficult case. At one point, my colleague told him that this patient was panicking at the analyst's impending long holiday. He had tried all kinds of interpretations about separation anxiety, envy, disillusionment, hatred, punishment—but the patient remained anxious and, clearly, suicidal. The senior analyst discussed these interpretations, but eventually suggested that my colleague might give his patient a photo of himself. Obviously, my colleague was surprised and mentioned the supervisor's insistence on the exclusiveness of interpretations in the analysis of any patients. "Oh, well, you don't really think that we put on paper all that we do in the consulting room, do you?" was the reply. Perhaps, along similar lines, there may be many analysts who might admit to episodes of touching their patients? It is a simple fact that the vast majority of practitioners do not recount or publish the details of their clinical work.

Considering the few accounts of touching that I have read, I am left with the impression that some analysts consider the actual or possible touching of the patient an exceptional event and try very hard to explain the reasons why they did or refused to do this.

Other analysts, however, seem to argue that here is a significant, valuable, effective technical paradigm and, accordingly, present theoretical justifications that would give legitimacy to their technique. I want to make it quite explicit that I do not have any doubts about the sincerity of their arguments or the ethical correctness of their practices. This would hold for Winnicott, as much as for any other colleague who decides to follow his footsteps.

However, I would strongly urge any of my students *never* to touch their patient. I do not consider shaking hands a type of touching and, if some exceptional circumstance leads to the analyst's body touching the patient's body, again I would not see this as anything more than an accident. If an example is called for, we have situations where patient and analyst have to climb stairs to reach the consulting room. If whoever is in front trips up and is about to fall, I would take it for granted that the person behind should hold the one in front and prevent his/her getting hurt. However, if the patient *asks* the analyst to hold his/her hands, I believe this has to be treated in the same way as any other request, i.e., considering its meaning in the context of the analytic situation. In a rather simplistic way, if the patient says, "You cannot imagine how I am feeling. I do wish you would let me hold your hands!", I would see this as an attempt to gauge the analyst's repertoire of communication abilities. The request can only arise because the patient has learnt that this is an analyst who does not use his body as an instrument of understanding or making contact. Agreeing to hold hands immediately signifies a new departure and I would argue that it may be very difficult for the patient to put into words his interpretation of the analyst's behaviour. We like to urge the analyst to be consistent and I would agree that there is a difference between consistency and rigidity. Nevertheless, any departure from the analyst's normal posture poses the danger of the patient, first, questioning his motives, and, second, wondering what other departures may eventually take place.

If, however, we have an analyst who does believe in physical contact in the work with a patient, then the issue of the patient asking for it surely should never arise. It is for the analyst to decide the moment when he touches or holds the patient's hands, head or other body parts.

It is important to remember that touching is not a common feature of British mores and this heightens the possibility that any touching may be misinterpreted by the patient. All considered, I repeat my advice to any students: a patient's request for touching is a matter for understanding, not for obliging.

I would like to conclude with another story. Eva Rosenfeld (personal communication, 1963), a most admired analyst, was in analysis with Melanie Klein in the 1940s. One day she reported having heard that a close relative had been killed by the Nazis. Mrs Rosenfeld was very distressed, indeed. The session came to the end and, as Mrs Rosenfeld got up from the couch, trying to get control of her balance, Mrs Klein suggested she should sit for a while in the waiting room and have a cup of tea that she offered to prepare. I have always seen this as a most telling example of the fact that whatever the transference makes of us, patient and analyst, we remain human beings. There is no harm in demonstrating our human solidarity with the pain of another person, but this makes sense when done spontaneously, not under the guise of psychodynamic conceptualizations. In other words, I do not think that it is important to touch a patient to show him/her that we care for his pain. If we do share it, our voice and demeanour will convey it and if we do not truly share it, our touching will still feel technical, not spontaneous.

# CHAPTER THREE

# Symbolic understanding of tactile communication in psychotherapy

*Camilla Bosanquet*

There has been considerable constructive dialogue between Freudians and Jungians since the rift between them in 1913. But one of the issues not discussed until recently is the issue of touch and tactile communication. Freud, after giving up hypnosis, when he would put his hand on his patient's forehead, devised his technique of abstinence with the therapist acting as a blank screen. As he puts it, analysts should "... model themselves ... on the surgeon, who puts aside all his feelings ..." (Freud, 1912e, p. 115). However, he also says,

> ... I am well advised ... to call these rules 'recommendations' and not to claim any unconditional acceptance for them. The extraordinary diversity of the psychical constellations concerned ... oppose any mechanization of the technique ... a course of action that is as a rule justified may at times prove ineffective, whilst one that is usually mistaken may ... lead to the desired end. [Freud, 1913c, p. 123]

Among other reasons, seeing libido as largely aggressive and sexual drives, he was afraid sexual encounters between analyst and patient would be enacted and his method would be repudiated as allowing free sexual licence. Ferenczi's more liberal behaviour was anathema to him; touching was therefore prohibited, and still is in psychoanalytic circles, despite the adoption of object relations theory and emphasis on the importance of the relationship between analyst and patient. Freud saw his method as essentially scientific and declared he wanted nothing to do with magic or religion.

Jung, on the other hand, was comfortable in the realm of religion. In his view, libido had a much broader dimension than sex and aggression, and included religion. He regarded the relationship between therapist and patient as paramount. As he puts it,

> . . . the relation between doctor and patient remains a personal one within the impersonal framework of professional treatment. . . . the whole being of the doctor as well as that of his patient plays its part. In the treatment there is an encounter between two irrational factors, that is to say, between two persons who are not fixed and determinable quantities but who bring with them, besides their more or less clearly defined fields of consciousness, an indefinitely extended sphere of non-consciousness. Hence the personalities of doctor and patient are often infinitely more important for the outcome of the treatment than what the doctor says and thinks . . . [Jung, 1931, p. 71]

Or, put more extravagantly, "For two personalities to meet is like mixing two different chemical substances: if there is any combination at all, both are transformed" (Jung, 1931, p. 71). There is no clear prohibition on touching.

As Mario Jacoby (1986, p. 115) puts it, "Among Jungians, where the restrictions in the analytic relationship are fewer and less well defined, there is all the same—and rightly—a warning against using body contact in an indiscriminate way". He adds, ". . . impulses to touch must stem clearly enough from the syntonic [in tune] aspects of countertransference . . . and must feel 'right' . . ." (p. 119).

States have long been recognized, in both Freudian and Jungian schools, where classical analysis is not adequate. Various terms have been used to describe these states and methods of coping with them, e.g., "the level of the basic fault" (Balint, 1968); or states "where delusion persists" Little (1966), who refers to these cases as needing "adaptations" or "parameters". Winnicott (1955) uses the term "management". In these states, tokens and touching are allowed but are not considered, by some, to be part of the analytic process.

Mario Jacoby (1986) supports Greene's (2001) thesis that Freud's view was a patriarchal one, whereas Ferenczi, Balint, Winnicott and others had a matriarchal view and recognized that some patients with very early damage needed some maternal caring. Touching could then be seen symbolically between mother and baby and would often be soothing rather than sexually exciting. Greene (2001) adds that, unlike therapists who work directly with the body, a Jungian training enables the symbolic understanding of tactile contact.

I will describe a fragment of analysis in which touching played an important part.

## Case history

Mavis was a missionary who started seeing me in 1962. She had kept all her feelings under tight control as she joined ever more rigid Evangelical circles within the Church. Finally, when on leave in England among her more liberal friends, she realized what was happening to her, questioned her more rigid beliefs and felt an urge to become alive.

She then became depressed, felt infantile, dependent and suicidal. For the first time she gave up and refused to go back to Africa when her leave ended. She sought professional help.

Mavis had had a difficult birth. She did not know the details, or whether she was in a breech or vertex position, but labour was prolonged and forceps were used. Her arms were damaged in some way, resulting in a condition resembling an Erb's palsy in that they were rotated inwards and backwards and she could not move them. But, unlike the treatment for Erb's palsy, her arms were apparently tied to her sides for the first few weeks of her life. A photograph taken of her at three months showed her still with her arms in this position.

She could not therefore use her hands to put them in her mouth, suck her fingers, explore or pummel the breast or to explore and identify herself. I will refer to this again later.

She had no memories of feeling held and she remembered her mother's handling as rough and she was left feeling hurt and uncomfortable. In later life her mother would hug her in a frenzied way when she came back on leave and Mavis hated this.

She had a horror that anything she felt and expressed would go on for ever. There was no conception of rhythm or climax in this case, although she was aware that her physiological rhythm never failed. Her bowels and her periods were regular and always had been and this was important to her. She had discovered only recently, however, from her mother, that for the first three weeks of her life she had had a nurse who insisted on her feeding for a full twenty minutes from each breast, and she had often been in great pain with vomiting, diarrhoea, and wind.

Her other fear was of an explosion, a state of cataclysmic excitement which she felt had got to happen. I shall refer to it in this paper in these terms but between us we did not succeed in finding a word that fitted this fear.

This state seemed to be connected with her birth experiences. She had two prevailing fantasies of babies: one in which the baby was curled up and quiet but inside an amniotic sac so that it could not reach out or be reached, and the other of a baby with its limbs splayed out in all directions, damaged and out of control. She could not picture how the baby in the first fantasy could emerge, nor the disaster that damaged the baby in the second fantasy. Between the two states there seemed to have been this catastrophe or explosion that shattered all feeling of continuity.

No bridge or transition could be made across this break. In fact, all kinds of transitions began frightening her, whether they were simply transitions from holiday to work, driving from one place to another, or changing from one mood to another. Then she got tense and tended to get migraines.

These transitions seemed to be related to the birth process where the transition from life *in utero*—the amniotic sac of her fantasy—to the outside world was disrupted by damage and catastrophe.

In particular, when she had bodily feelings in relation to my body she became aware of vague feelings of excitement that turned to panic. She was convinced that both our bodies would get out of control in a state of—she could not picture what. There would be no awareness and our boundaries would be lost. It seemed a total annihilation and she could not picture anything beyond it.

So any expression of bodily feelings was terrifying because it would, she felt, inevitably go on for ever or pitch her into a cataclysmic explosion. I use the term bodily rather than sexual feeling because although it might start as a sexual feeling, it soon arouses these early components leading to a diffuse state of excitement and panic. Her frequent migraines seemed to be almost a realization of these fears. They usually came on after a period of relaxation, particularly on waking from a deep sleep, as though after she had had a feeling of being held and able to relax. She had a splitting headache that threatened to overwhelm her with pain. She vomited and this went on as if for ever—until a doctor could come and give her an injection. She had diarrhoea that did stop eventually, and as the migraine wore off she had a compulsion to talk and talk. Afterwards she felt depressed.

To go back to her hands; although they appeared normal they were weak and she had never felt they were an integral part of her. As a child—and still at times when worked up and frustrated—she would indulge in what her family called "patting". She would go to her room and pat two fingers of one hand on the clenched knuckles of the other. While doing this she would have fantasies of being on the other side of the obstacle; for example, being able to do what she wanted, having successfully fought with her parents; or able to take in what she read. In fact, life without her present difficulties.

The fantasies did not include the actual battle with the frustrating object, e.g., her parents, and the energy needed for this would be expended in the patting. This was a frenzied and exhausting exercise, it had no climax and she went on until she was tired out. When reading she would feel overwhelmed by the book and then have to start patting with the book. This consisted of rapid alternating movements of patting and turning the book round in her hand. It also went on until she finally stopped out of sheer exhaustion. It was an effort to break the book down into manageable proportions.

In this context I was reminded of Hoffer's article, "Mouth, hand and ego-integration" (1949, p. 50), that ". . . from intra-uterine life onward it [the hand] becomes closely allied to the mouth for the sake of relieving tension and within this alliance leads to the first achievement of the primitive ego". Mavis had never managed to relieve tension through her hands; her fears of cataclysmic excitement had no outlets for release. Her patting rituals were an unsuccessful attempt to relieve tension, but they led only to exhaustion.

In the same article Hoffer stresses a baby's need to be able to touch himself with his hands, and to feel the toucher as distinct from the touched and appreciate the difference, also the difference between touching himself and objects in the outside world. Spitz (1965) qualifies Hoffer's statements and regards the hand as only one of several means of libidinizing the body and separating the me from the not-me. Although Mavis was presumably able to do this in a limited way, it seems likely that her perceptions may have been distorted by the autonomous frightening feelings and destructive energy she felt to be in her hands. But this is getting speculative.

Mavis managed very well in the outside world. She had many friends and was competent and successful in her job, which was a responsible one.

Her social relationships felt unsatisfying to her because she was always searching for something deeper. Her friends, on the other hand, felt that their relationship with her was both deep and satisfying and could not understand why she was still in analysis.

As a child she had had a close friend of the same age. They used to play together all the time, cut each other's hair, explore each other's bodies and defy their respective parents. Mavis felt that in this friendship a healing process was starting in which she was becoming able to use and feel with her hands. This was shattered when war broke out and they were evacuated to different parts of the country. She was then eight years old. After this she patted frantically for some time.

In her analysis with me, at first she would talk to me apparently quite freely, but she achieved this by denying that I had a body. She could not remember between sessions what I looked like or what I was wearing. I was just a blur.

During a session she would suddenly become aware of my body and hers. Her talk would stop. She would then sit looking despondent and paralysed and no words made any difference. She was vaguely aware of unlocalized feelings in her body, but then a curtain of futility would come down and obscure them. Her main fears were that I would either turn on her, tell her she had had enough, that was the end, and leave her, or that my body would get out of control, in a state of cataclysmic excitement too. There would be no boundaries, no awareness. She couldn't picture what.

She tried with great efforts of will-power to overcome her frozen paralysis by sitting or lying in different places, on the couch, on the chair, on the floor. I moved around, too, but it made no difference. She could not break through it as she could not break through the amniotic sac of her fantasy. Occasionally she would make herself hold my hands and hold them silently for reassurance, but it did not help. I will say more about this later.

Mavis's life was divided into compartments. One of the divisions was between fantasying and doing. You could do things or you could have fantasies about doing them, but never both. It dawned on me that her fears of my body were so great, talking and interpreting seemed to make no difference, and that perhaps what she needed was to be able to touch me, to feel my body with her hands, to hold and play with my hands and to fantasize and verbalize her fantasies at the same time— to fantasize and to do.

I do not mean by this that everything she fantasized had to be possible in actuality but that some real doing with recognition and response on an instinctive level had to be possible before her fantasies could lead to symbolism and development. Without this her fantasies led only to increasing states of excitement that could not be discharged in action. This was coped with by an increasing degree of paralysis. I can imagine that without this she could have been merely repeating her early experience when she had had strong feelings in her hands that she could not discharge, and later developed fantasies about what they could do, but was unable to try any of them out because she could not actually move her hands and touch and grasp.

She wanted to come and hold my hands. So I gestured, "Well, why not?" She came and sat on the floor, snuggled up beside me and held my hands. She then let them go and said she supposed she could let my hands go really instead of having to hold on to them forever. She then held them again and was able to become more aware of the vague, diffuse feelings in her body and talk about them. It was only then that we managed to start breaking these feelings down into any definable sort of proportion.

She wanted me to hold her physically. When I did so she wriggled out and said nothing was any good. There was only one thing that really seemed to count and that was "the perfect gulp". She knew it was an ideal and could not really feel like that. But that was it; she had to stand out for it. I said I supposed that if her hands had been tied by her sides and she could not use them to get what she wanted, how she wanted, the gulp would have to be perfect. She said she was too frightened to think of using her hands, but she came back and held mine and sighed, then said that her sighs were efforts to blow away these feelings in her hands.

After she was able to take my hands and fantasize at the same time she was pleased, and said that what she had felt would inevitably be an explosion could instead be a steady learning process. It has been a learning process for both of us.

Touching and feeling things with her hands had always been a natural form of expression for her—objects, a sculpture, for example, animals and sick people whom she felt to be weaker than herself. On other occasions, too, when she felt the bond of reassurance and love was strong enough. But when she felt that her approach or the other person's response might be overwhelming she could not touch them. She pictured her hands completely out of control in some way and this was when inhibition set in and she became paralysed. The exciting and destructive feelings in her hands were too much.

Her friend who had helped her most before coming to me was a demonstrative person who naturally held hands with Mavis when talking to her. Mavis could only talk to her when she was holding her hands but it never satisfied her hungry infantile feelings and she despaired because she felt the holding must never stop. With me she felt touching was taboo; this was partly because she was aware of the charge of feeling in her hands that she had not felt so strongly with her friend. It had been reinforced, too, by reading psychoanalytic literature from which she had got the impression that touching was not a part of the analytical contract. She was afraid, too, that if she did touch me it might only be repeating the experience she had had with her friend, that she would not be able to absorb the feeling and let it be transformed as she put it; she would want to go on holding for ever.

The turning point came, she felt, when she was able to hold my hands and feel and talk about her bodily feelings at the same time. Before this, when she had silently held my hands, she had felt this as a break in what was going on between us, as though saying, "Please let me hold your hands for a bit then I will talk again." This was accepted, she felt, but it was a hindrance and separate from the rest of the interchange between us. Subsequently, touching with its accompanying feelings in her hands and body began to be a part of the communication and hence a more integral part of herself.

She had been learning in several obvious ways by being able to feel me and fantasize and recognize some of the feelings in her body and hands. She once shook me by the arm in a frenzy and was surprised to find that I felt pliable, whereas she had assumed that I would either feel rigid or break. Having felt this physically it occurred to her that this might be carried over into my general behaviour, that I would not say "no" in a rigid way or, alternatively, collapse, and also that I could be different from her in this way. She wanted to hold my hands and to look at me and at herself holding my hands, which she did.

She seemed to be learning, too, that in general nothing I did was right. For example, if I held her it was not right; she became aware that what she wanted was the perfect gulp, but more important was that when I did the wrong thing it was not catastrophically wrong. It seemed to be my failures of adjustment on a tactile level, as well as other levels, which were necessary to break up the cataclysm into manageable amounts of feeling and lead the way to a possibility of transitions.

Nevertheless, every step in the direction of learning had its hazards. Each time she had felt there had been some real communication between us she became convinced that next time I would say, "Well, you have had that now. That's enough," and she felt hopeless. Fundamentally, all exchanges and expressions of feeling were rationed. This assumption was her defence against excess—the explosion. She began to be able to recognize that this was her assumption and not my attitude. She felt that she tried almost to bring this explosion on in order to deal with it quickly and try to control it, instead of letting the infant inside her grow at its own pace, as she put it.

Words had been of little use in the past because she would have to wait until the feeling had gone out of them before she said them and then it was no good. Some expression of feeling seemed to be allowed into her words if she could hold me and in this way get some actual recognition and acknowledgement of her feelings and fantasies.

The migraines I described earlier became more linked with the bodily feelings she had while she was with me—feelings of her body being torn apart from inside and something trying to get out. She was afraid of being split apart. Her migraines to begin with seemed to be states of disintegration, a shattering followed by an almost complete detachment afterwards when she could only describe what she had felt like, but could not re-experience it.

Later, they came to be experienced more as states of de-integration. She had felt more able to feel held both during her migraines and at other times. There was "a bottom to the world", as she put it. This feeling of being held came out of the experience of holding me and realizing that an essential factor in feeling held is to be able to hold and grasp the person or object which is holding you so that it is not catastrophic if their hold is not quite right.

There followed an interim period between her migraines and normal state, when she felt opened up with a heightened awareness. This state fluctuated between one of hope and new possibilities and one of nausea and depression. During one of these periods while she was with me she became conscious of a feeling of space round her in which she felt she could manoeuvre and play. She fantasized that the mat was covered with toys and hoped that I would not sweep them away so that they could still be there the next time she came. Also, she stopped being overwhelmed by the pressing problems of work that were going to greet her the following day. Instead she felt she could push them on to the next day where they belonged and enjoy her freedom while she had it. This seemed to me to have the features of cycles of de-integration and integration and at the same time the beginning of a transitional area, and possibly of a bridge, an awareness of transition through the gap or explosion of her birth experience; the transition from the amniotic sac to the outside world where she could reach out and be reached.

I realize that in my effort to highlight this aspect of her analysis I have given a very one-sided picture. But this is the part I wanted to emphasize in this paper. For the rest, there had been six years of analysis before we reached this level. Her initial attitude, that she had so much to be thankful for and others were less fortunate than herself, wore thin, and strong feelings of resentment and envy broke through. Other people got married and she could not, her friends went away for expensive holidays and she could not afford to. We tried to analyse her envy but it persisted because her underlying problems persisted, making it impossible for her to have anything. Consequently she felt envious and the vicious circle continued.

## Development

When one considers the development of a baby, it seems to me likely that, in some cases with severe early deprivation or distortion, the experience of touching, holding, snuggling, and bumping against may have to be repeated, although symbolically, but it is a question of finding the most appropriate basis for this.

In the early stages, a baby speaks with its whole body. Its movements are incomplete and undifferentiated and these have to be interpreted and completed by the mother. It is his mother's response to these that helps to reduce his whole undifferentiated body movements to gestures. Touching is one of the primary means of communication. It can be regarded as a basis upon which other forms of communication are built up. Tactile experiences are combined with, or in some cases superseded by, later perceptions, for example seeing and hearing. A newborn baby has to find the nipple by a combined sense of touch and kinaesthetic sensations. This method is superseded when it begins to see and focus. It then finds the nipple by looking for it.

If these earlier tactile perceptions and behaviour have not been adequately responded to and confirmed by the mother, then there may be a contradiction or distortion between these and later acquired perceptions, namely seeing and hearing. This is an over-simplification, but Frank (1957, p. 230) suggests that, "perhaps many of the personality disorders . . . are due to deprivation of essential tactile experience and to the establishment of signs and symbols upon inadequate or disordered tactile experience". He also suggests that where a baby's tactile experiences have been limited, he will have to wait until his capacity for visual and auditory recognition has developed before he can communicate effectively. These symbols, what the baby sees and hears, will appear to him more arbitrary if his perceptions have not previously been built up on an experiential basis of tactile communication. These children, ". . . may be more dependent than other children on the authority of parents who define and impose these signs and symbols" (Frank, 1957, p. 230).

Provided these early responses and experiences have been adequate, there is by now a well developed pre-verbal communication system in which the mother interprets and reciprocates her baby's behaviour. Verbal communication begins to develop out of this pre-verbal matrix. Here again, if pre-verbal communications are limited or distorted there will be difficulties with verbal communication.

## Regression

It is hard to know to what extent early development is paralleled in states of regression. In regression early perceptions and responses must be contaminated by later experiences and developments. As Winnicott (1957, p. 111) says, "To some extent 'deeper and deeper' does of course imply 'earlier and earlier', but only to a limited extent . . . in our analytic patients there has been a fusion of early with later elements."

In states of regression the patient allows the infantile part of him to be lived through in his analysis while his adult part can still function in the outside world and enable him to lead a responsible life in the world.

The infantile part of him has its own language. Words have little or changed meaning. As Balint says,

> . . . they have become lifeless, repetitious, and stereotyped; they strike one as an old worn-out gramophone record, with the needle running endlessly in the same groove . . . this is often equally true about the analyst's interpretations; during these periods they, too, seem to be running endlessly in the same groove. The analyst then discovers to his despair and dismay that, in these periods, there is no point whatever in going on interpreting the patient's verbal communications. [Balint, 1968, p. 175]

On the other hand, the analyst's tone of voice, his movements and expressions become all-important. There is no sense of time or continuity, and time between sessions can feel infinite. Separation is difficult and there can be a longing for physical contact.

The analyst will have to provide a good holding environment, a symbolic equivalent to a mother's care of a baby. As Little (1966, p. 483) states, "In patients where delusion prevails, the patient . . . needs concrete and actual bodily realities. When these have been found, they can be linked with words by the analyst and brought within reach of interpretation."

Balint (1968, p. 144) differentiates between what he calls benign and malignant regressions. In the benign form of regression, he states that the aim is recognition. "What the patient expects is not so much a gratification by an external action, but a tacit consent to use the external world in a way that would allow him to get on with his internal problems." Whereas malignant regression, ". . . is aimed at a gratification of instinctual cravings. What the patient seeks is an external event, an action by his object" (*ibid*.). This latter form can lead to addiction, the need for further gratification.

It seems to me that this must be a quantitative rather than a qualitative distinction and that there might be a continuum between the two categories. A regression will appear more benign when the patient is in a relatively calm state, with an ego functioning quite well so that he can make use of his object, than when he is in the sway of disturbing emotions with relatively weak ego function. But this is only a question on my part.

Whether the overall impression of a state of regression in a patient is benign or malignant by this definition seems to depend on which end of the continuum the patient is predominantly functioning, and whether he can transfer his learned experience from his calmer states to his more disturbed states.

Mavis mainly needed a recognition of, and consent to, some of her basic needs. I think we often mislead ourselves by talking of gratifications, when all we are doing is recognizing and completing a communication so that there is a possibility of further development.

Both Margaret Little and Balint imply that provision of pre-verbal and actual bodily realities should only happen in the state of delusion, or what Balint calls the state of harmonious "mix up" before the verbal phase is established, and that after this analysis should be carried out on a verbal level. But I think that there are occasions when it is vital that the two processes should be allowed to go on at the same time, so that these different modes of communication can be received by the analyst and responded to both verbally and pre-verbally, with some link up or synchronization of the different communication channels. At different times during the session one form is more dominant than the other and the synchronization between the two varies.

With Mavis, verbal communication was quite fluent until she suddenly became aware of my body and her bodily feelings. Then it would stop completely and any communication there was would be pre-verbal, looking, sighing, curling up. At other times, and particularly when she was holding me, there could be some link up of the two. Before this her talking stopped because of a fear of her intense feelings getting into her talk. The expression of feeling by talking would then be too much. Consequently her talk stopped until her feelings subsided, leaving her words safe but ineffectual. So-called parameters, by which I include touching, are regarded as endangering the analytic process and, if used inappropriately, they can. But it seems to me that when used appropriately they can enhance the analytic process. As a colleague of mine once said, it can "loosen the feelings". It can lead to a feeling of greater understanding and trust and hence enable the patient to explore deeper hitherto unconscious feelings. Without this, the patient can feel stuck, as was the case with Mavis.

There are links with Bowlby's work on attachment behaviour. Balint, Winnicott, and other Freudians were proponents of the school of object relations. This refocused Freud's theory of a pleasure-seeking drive: as one writer put it, "person seeking", rather than "pleasure seeking". This involves a close relationship between mother and baby and, although not identical, between analyst and regressed patient. Originally, there was a wide gap between Bowlby's observations of mothers and babies, from which he introduced his theory of attachment behaviour, and the psychoanalyst's view of infancy from the inside experience of regressed patients.

Bowlby maintained that attachment behaviour was distinct from feeding or sexual behaviour and functioned as a protection from predators and was therefore essential for the survival of the species. Both lines of research point to the vital importance of a close relationship between analyst and patient. In this context, Pedder (1976, pp. 491) questions ". . . whether it can ever be appropriate to gratify a patient's wish for physical contact with the analyst, e.g., the wish to hold a hand, during a period of regression in analysis".

Jung felt that the close relationship between analyst and patient was paramount. Although he may have known little of the experiences of regressed patients then, the theme of object relations and importance of relationships is vital today.

Recent research in the field of neuroscience suggests that a significant part of brain development relies on the registering of early experience through physical contact. Stern (1990, p. 99) remarks that, "The ultimate magic of attachment is touch. And the magic enters through the skin." He adds that the skin is the largest sensory organ in the body and skin contact has a large representation in the brain.

## Touching habits in society

Touching inhibitions are introduced at various stages of development; initially in infancy, longings for tactile contact that are not met and satisfied become repudiated as a defence against the pain of longing. This leads to an aversion to touching later on. So do early traumatic experiences of touching.

As the baby becomes more active, in the interests of safety, its mother's attitude changes from one of pleasure and encouragement of its explorations to admonitions against touching. "Don't touch" must be one of the most common injunctions a baby receives from its mother when it starts crawling about.

Later there are more obvious sexual connotations. Small children are no longer allowed to touch and explore their mother's body and very often not the genital areas of their own. To be told not to touch is not then a simple injunction but becomes loaded with overtones of disgust and fear.

Many adults have great unsatisfied yearnings to touch and be touched. This may be felt, but is sometimes denied, in which case touching is actively avoided. It always seems to me that one of our main reasons for keeping pets is because fondling and touching pets is freely sanctioned. But of course, touch can be a disturber. Some people become furious and jump as if stung if they are touched during a conversation.

In general, people have been becoming more openly demonstrative but, contrasted with this, increased awareness of the prevalence of sexual abuse, and the damage it causes, has resulted in strict rules being drawn up to protect children, and, in the current climate, we are all more vulnerable to accusations of inappropriate touching. Teachers are afraid to touch children under their care. Some do not dare to put an arm around a small child who is distressed and crying, or to clean up a child who has messed himself. Almost any form of touching can be construed as abuse if the person being touched wants to make it seem so. How do we steer our way through these difficulties?

## Touching in the analytic setting

Until recently, there seems to have been very little discussion on the subject of touch, and I think many questions need to be asked.

My own interest in tactile communication grew from a demonstration given by Alexander Lowen from New York. His theories (Lowen, 1967) were based on Reich's (1933) concept of character analysis and muscular armouring. The basis of this is that the repression of feelings involves muscular contraction and tension that suppresses the feeling and inhibits the accompanying action. Certain muscle tensions get built in the course of character development, and he had found that if these can be released by touching, massage, and movements there may be an accompanying release of repressed feelings and fantasies. He regarded this process as an essential part of analysis.

Lowen came over to London in 1967 and gave a demonstration. A group of four of us, three psychoanalysts and myself, were impressed by some of his methods, and, particularly by his way of touching patients, moving and talking as an integral part of communication, which included fantasying and interpreting. From our background of analytical training we could not wholly adopt Lowen's methods, but we wanted to see if we could adapt some of his techniques and incorporate them into the analysis of some patients, whom we felt we had been unable to help on a verbal level.

These patients were particularly ones who had early pre-verbal disturbances and who either felt stuck because their yearning for tactile contact was so great or, like Mavis, had become more aware of their intense bodily feelings but with no opportunity to discharge them in action in our setting. The only way they could cope with them was by sitting feeling frozen and paralysed.

I agree with Jacoby (1986) when he talks of occasions when touching could be seen as a facilitating response rather than an intrusion, even though the patient has not initiated it. He talks of patients who,

> ... tend to get temporarily into a kind of "depressive freeze", a "frozen" state where their own feelings—let alone persons of the outside world—are not reachable. ... I felt in certain instances that

these patients needed my active help in trying to find them in their prisons. . . . Thus the impulse to reach the patient by some direct physical touch seems appropriate. However such a move needs the "right moment". . . . I would risk such a move only with a few carefully selected patients in moments when it just felt right. [M. Jacoby, 1986, pp. 121–122]

I think that originally when Mavis had held my hands, other forms of communication stopped. There seemed to be a basic feeling that either we talk or we touch and hold, and only in a few situations does it seem natural to combine the two. This seemed to make touching more dangerous; perhaps there is a fear of being drawn into something that cannot be analysed or integrated. The difficulty with Mavis may have been, too, that she was not then in a state to integrate the two. It may have been my difficulty in integrating the two as well. But later, when we were able to integrate this touching and interpretation, it was dynamic and things started moving as I have described.

I have been interested to hear the comments of other analysts and psychoanalysts when I have asked for their views on touching as a form of communication in some analytical situations and whether they use it. For Freudian psychoanalysts, touch has always been prohibited except for particular situations described as parameters or management. For Jungian analysts it has never been prohibited, but there are many who say they would never touch a patient under any circumstances. Reasons given are sometimes personal, such as that the analyst would not feel safe, and this I respect. But often reasons do not seem to have been thought through and instances are quoted when touching would be quite inappropriate and would fail or lead to disaster. There is sometimes a flavour of, "There you are. You see!" The sort of reasons given are that touching is not symbolic, it deprives the patient of space, it would be an intrusion, particularly in patients who have a history of abuse. Some saw it only as a sexual interchange and stated that it was a pity to throw overboard such a well worked out form of therapy as psychoanalysis by allowing a sexual relationship. But then, if there is a sexual element, can it not be understood and accepted and—if necessary—interpreted, as with any other interpretation?

Of the analysts who had allowed touching, their experience was that it took place at the end of the session on the way to the door. There seem to me to be disadvantages in this because touching, which is quite often the most fundamental and meaningful form of contact, then tends to get suspended in a kind of limbo, even though it can to some extent be talked about and brought into the subsequent session. I feel, in general, that if there is to be tactile contact it should be during the session and should be an integral part of it.

Another reason for making it part of the session is to include the often harder problem of stopping touching, letting go. It is easy at the door because there is a natural break, but it is only during the session that it is possible to pick up patients' feelings of anger and rejection when they have to let go. Mavis suggested this to me. She would hold my hands just as she went out of the door. One day she said to me, "Well this is no good because there is a natural end, and what I am afraid of is things going on for ever. I must see if I can hold your hands before it is time to go and then see if I can let go of them."

This reminded me of a man who was in analysis with me for seven years. The first part of that time he had seen me as a witch, and much time was spent working through this and his numerous other problems. When he was about to terminate his analysis, he had a great urge to put his arms round me and hug me before he finally left. He did not know why it mattered so much and neither did I. Finally he did hug me. He was surprised and relieved to find that my body felt soft, like a girl, and not leathery like a witch. He then gave me a box of Black Magic chocolates which we both ate, ascertained the ages of my children and that I was securely married, and left satisfied. During the course of his analysis, he had got married himself and they were expecting a baby. Wanting to hug me was partly sadness in parting. However, it seemed that having worked through his fear of witches, people had become real for him on most levels, but he had to verify this on a tactile level before he could be satisfied.

When a patient stretches out a hand for support or comfort at times of great pain and stress, or when he asks to hold the analyst's hand, does the analyst feel free to "allow" this and, if not, what were his reasons in that particular situation?

In states of regression, Margaret Little (1966, p. 480), writing of parameters or management, says, "A new set of experiences of good enough mothering needs to be supplied before the ego can become accessible to verbal interpretation," and which, "allows the individual patient a greater freedom to direct the analyst to suit his personal needs".

Since the publication of an earlier version of this paper in 1970, there has been a move in the Society of Analytical Psychology, without much discussion, against touching, and our code of ethics now has a clause: "Physical contact should be avoided unless, in the analyst's judgement, it is clinically indicated, such as, if the patient is a danger to himself or others." This clause, in some form, is now in most analytic organizations' code of ethics, largely because awareness of sexual abuse is in everyone's minds at the present time and strict rules have been drawn up in an attempt to safeguard against it. I feel this move is an indication to discuss the subject of tactile contact more, rather than less, as analysts need to become more aware of the needs and dangers associated with it. Analysis, after all, is about letting unconscious feelings and behaviour become conscious and this applies to analysts as well as to patients.

Regarding the effect of an official prohibition on touching, I imagine that if touching is officially prohibited it will not have been extensively explored. Does the prohibition constitute an acceptable boundary? Or is it experienced at times as an interference? I wonder if the prohibition makes it harder for an analyst to respond to the patient's imaginative and symbolic touching.

When I talk of not allowing tactile contact, I am referring to situations both when it is explicitly not allowed and when it is implicitly not allowed, when there is a confusion of signals because the analyst is not clear in his own mind whether he can really take part in it or not. He may then imply that he is willing but his bodily attitude and movements may contradict this. This is both confusing and rejecting for the patient and can lead to a block in the analysis. It has been suggested to me that perhaps we should not make any interpretation on a bodily level unless we feel in ourselves that we could carry it out in actuality.

My thesis is that, as analysts, we should discuss the whole question of touching/tactile contact openly and fully and dispel the assumption that it almost inevitably leads to an enactment of a sexual relationship. This is not saying we should all touch, but only let us discuss the indications for and against it. My view is that it can be part of the ongoing analytic process rather than an interference, particularly when it can be a soothing experience in states where the analytic process is blocked by excessive anxiety, and in regressed states where it can help to establish an early relationship and early boundary between analyst and patient. In any case, it can only be a symbolic expression of what the patient wants. It can only carry the meaning.

# CHAPTER FOUR

# No touch please—we're British psychodynamic practitioners

*Valerie Sinason*

> It is my contention that one of the worst professional ethical violations is to permit current risk-management principles to take precedence over human interventions.
>
> (Lazarus, 1994, p. 255)

> To care for people is more important than to care for ideas, which can be good servants but bad masters.
>
> (Guntrip, 1971, p. 27)

A baby is crying. Everybody looks around. Louder than the traffic, the sirens of police cars, the shouting of street vendors, the cry of the baby pierces all the busy shoppers. Heads turn round. You can almost hear the thought bubbles bursting out of the myriad heads. "Pick it up! Please pick it up!", "Stop that noise", "Mothers these days!", "Spoilt brat! I'll give it something to cry for . . ." There are frowns, looks of sympathy, tuts. And then the mother lifts the baby out of the pram. The baby is no longer an "it" but a girl. The mother holds her affectionately and kisses her. The crying has stopped. The mother strokes her cheeks, her heads, her arms. Her voice is gentle and loving. Everyone is settled again. Everyone's internal baby, past frozen baby, has been touched. The world is safe again.

Every shopping street, every park replays this scene thousands of times. The script varies very little. We are brought to vibrant life through touch and in its absence we wilt and shrivel. Orphanage babies died through lack of touch (Spitz, 1945). On the island of Leros in Greece, children and adults with severe learning disabilities lost the use of their legs; left lying on their beds, they had no one to walk to, to reach out to. Hunter and Struve (1997) usefully sum up the measurable beneficial physiological changes that occur through touch: from massaged premature infants gaining weight 45% more rapidly than others, to severely ill patients whose heart rate and respiratory rate improved when a nurse held their hands.

Touch is a lifesaver and a life giver. However, as with any basic human need, it has its traumatic side. The old colloquialism "touched in the head" meaning "mad", shows a deep-rooted understanding of touch gone wrong. Physical, sexual, and emotional abuse lead the way, together with emotional and physical deprivation. Offering a hand is a friendly gesture to some, or a dangerous intrusion, or an irrelevant appendage, depending on the person or the context.

It is therefore not surprising that psychoanalysis and psychoanalytically derived verbal therapies have a complex history in trying to come to terms with physical touch. Freud, in his work with Breuer, realized the sexual transference could be exacerbated unhelpfully through the method of touch he employed. He found his own solution. The patient was to lie on the couch not seeing the psychoanalyst's face. Succeeding generations with a Western culture added to this and a guideline turned into a concrete monolith. Touch, even a handshake in some analytic cultures, was "incompetent and criminal" (Menninger, 1958).

Orbach (2003a) brilliantly points out that while psychoanalysis has had a relatively recent rapprochement with attachment theory, the fact that attachment includes actual touch, physical proximity, is disavowed. There is an over-valuation of mind "as a kind of moral superego to feeling and bodies" (Orbach, 2003a, p. 6).

Later anthropologists will be able to throw more light on why our current psychodynamic culture is so fascinated by the brain and neuroscience and why there is a possible over-valuation occurring on top of a true inter-collegiate reciprocity. While psychotherapies are perhaps undergoing a paradigm shift secretly, drawing on the neurosciences, paediatric research, and developmental psychology as cover (Sinason, 1995), there is also a buzz around this subject. In current slang, the topic is "sexy". It is safe for mind and brain to be sexy because Cartesian dualism is alive in our culture, our use of psychoanalytic thinking, and ourselves. Mind is cognitive. It might have a physical home that scientists know about, but it is safely non-sexual. It is out of range for ordinary touch. No touch please, we are psychoanalytically orientated, has become a commandment. To cope with the privileged access to the mind of the client, a split has been made that excludes the body.

The level of the split might be hard to see at first, as language is so full of body parts! Look at this sentence from Klein (1932, p. 111): "On the other hand, it is still unexplained why, particularly in the latency period, the child's struggle against masturbation is at its height". In raising a conceptual question about an activity that takes place usually using the hand, Klein brings in a figure of speech "on the other hand". The word "masturbation", as a Latinate word, distances itself psycho-linguistically from touch, while "hand" is the simple word. Look at Winnicott's use of the "holding" environment. Every theoretical group within psychotherapy uses metaphors for touch, containment, even-handedness.

As babies and toddlers we learn the world through touch. Oral language comes later. Does that make us denigrate touch as being more primitive? How do we fine-tune according to our own resources, our clients and our colleague community? What are the fears around abstinence and neutrality?

## Abstinence and neutrality

It was Freud (1915a) who considered it a fundamental principle that the patient's need and longing should be allowed to persist in order to allow working through rather than answering those needs. He saw this as part of the analyst's neutrality (1913c), a position of "sympathetic understanding" (1915a) rather than judgement or action. Touch, as gratifying a longing, was problematic. Ferenczi, whose pioneering work with trauma victims involved touch, and whose technical queries on this subject aided Freud's crystallization of concepts of neutrality and abstinence, had a relationship with a patient. However, as shown by work from Glen Gabbard (1995) and POPAN, the Prevention of Professional Abuse Network, sexual connections between patients and analysts exist across all kinds of treatments, whether they involve touch or not. Could it be that each rule that is made as a consequence of one problem creates new ones?

## Work with children

In the consulting room children fall over, they climb, they cry, they run, they wet themselves, they need the toilet. Boundaries are not so fixed as with adult patients. We can interpret and hold physically at the same time.

### Feeling and interpreting the kiss-punch

Marie, aged eight, was sexually abused by her father from earliest childhood. Her mother was emotionally cut off from her. She saw her father as the only person who loved her. She was a source of worry and discomfort at her junior school because of her highly sexualized behaviour. Staff were aware of feeling physically sickened by her behaviour and struggled with primitive wishes to retaliate.

In the therapy room, she threw herself on to my lap and would press against me. I could comment on how little Marie longed to be held but could not imagine it was possible without something sexual because that was what she was used to. I could verbalize my countertransference by commenting that it felt like a kiss-punch, something that conveyed two messages at the same time and perhaps that what was what she felt when people held her.

To have not allowed her actual physical contact would have been to re-enact, in the transference, the role of the cold withdrawn mother, an abdication of analytic neutrality. It also mattered to her that her sense of herself as repellent, as the carrier of damage, could be managed in reality without rejection.

There are many cases involving touch where the child is brilliantly communicating through behaviour the internal and external environmental mixture that is causing pain. A child with a physically disabled parent who cannot provide physical holding, and does not succeed in providing a substitute mental holding, can equally be hurt by a therapy that does not "catch hold" physically as well as mentally.

## Joan

Joan, aged eleven, had a mother with muscular dystrophy and no father. She was failing at school after a long history of falls and "clumsiness". She needed me to be the one who could not catch anything in the therapy room and took a particular delight in leaping from chairs and falling to show that I, like her mother, could not hold her. To catch her would be to provoke a terrible sense of disloyalty to her mother, and to fail to catch her would exonerate her mother but add to her fear that there was no other way. She was beginning to fail at school and, several years before GCSEs, was already worrying about which subjects to "drop". She was unpopular at games and called "Butterfingers".

In the poem "Caught out" (Sinason, 1988), I write of such a child whose mother could not hold her because of a physical disability. In identification with that mother, she too was dropping everything.

CAUGHT OUT

> Butterfingers hides
> By the crumbling arch of the toilets
> Around her, poor Jenny lies a-weeping
> The farmer wants a wife
> And the chosen ones leap, jostle
> Their plaits like skipping-ropes, shining
>
> And high above everyone
> The balls flying higher than windows

Bouncing and zooming and spinning
In the language she never learned

She opens her hands like a prayer
And prays for a ball to choose her
For its own particular blessing
She cannot bear the syntax of reach, catch

And while the other girls catch balls, badges
The glittering prizes of play
She learns the alphabet of destruction

She is learning how to drop cities
How to let times tables, amoebae
And rain forests disappear
Through the cracks between her fingers

She will drop
So much faster than they can catch
She won't see she hasn't caught anything
She won't know
Except, of course, she does
And knows
She has caught,
Herself,
*Out.*

Our task in the therapy room was to verbally and metaphorically address these issues, at the same time as physically looking into the implications of being caught or not caught.

In one session, as she made her customary long leap from a chest of drawers to a sofa, her foot caught on the wooden frame at the side of the sofa, tilting her over. I rushed to catch her, preventing her falling.

She stayed frozen in my arms. I lowered her gently. She stood frozen on the ground. Then she slowly moved to the couch and sat on it. I returned to my chair. The silence continued. She looked at me with an ashen face and then screamed in the loudest voice. "It's not fair. She couldn't do that." And then she cried.

I remained in my seat. It was a moment where no touch would have been right. "You are right. It's not fair," I said softly. "Even if she had wanted to hold you, even if every bit of her longed to she could not."

Joan nodded.

We both knew it was her actual mother that was being spoken about.

It was after this session that a dramatic transformation took place. Her leaping stopped. She began to throw dolls into the air and catch them. Then balls. For a while she wanted to learn juggling. For the next six months there was a manic period of showing she could catch everything and then she settled down to her studies and to a therapy that required no further physical touch.

## Work with adults

I would like to focus on clients who have gone through extreme experiences of trauma and disability.

## Disability: Carole

One young woman with a severe learning disability came for a therapy assessment after a sadistic rape in her day centre. She described a care worker raping her and then mocking her. "I wouldn't go near you again with a bargepole," she shouted, aping a sadistic male voice. She sat in the corner of the room as far away as she could from me, her coat still on and her arms wrapped around her to make a double protection.

She looked disgusted—her face still in identification with her abuser to cover the enormity of the helplessness, pain and humiliation she felt.

I wondered aloud whether she did not want to go anywhere near me because she was sitting so far away from me. Was I too disgusting for her to sit nearer to? She looked shocked. "It's not you. Really. You're all right," she said. Her body stance became more relaxed and her arms fell to her sides.

"Are you sure?" I asked. "You are not just saying that to make me feel all right?" She burst out laughing. "I'm not rude," she said. "I don't think you stink. You are not like the people in my day centre—all smelly."

I asked what she felt about being near smelly people and she said she did not like it. "Especially the men. And they leave the toilets disgusting."

I asked her if she would feel worried if I moved nearer to her. Would that make her worry about me stinking?

"No," she said. "I can touch your hand. Then you will know I think you are OK."

I moved to a chair nearer to the couch and very slowly held out my hand. She reached it and touched it firmly. Then she took her coat off. "It is nice and warm in here," she said. "It is cold outside."

This brief transcript shows the way touch was useful in alleviating a sense of disgust. No further touched happened in this patient's therapy, which then went on for two years.

Disgust is often evoked literally and metaphorically around the topic of shit (Anglo-Saxon) or faeces/defecation. In the UK we have borrowed loan words from another language to hide the simpler Anglo-Saxon word.

### Disgust and Leros

Here is a concrete example of where touch matters. It was on the island of Leros in Greece, before the images of the abandonment and abuse of the disabled children of Romania. The old fascist-built asylums were being opened up, thanks to the courage of a psychiatrist and psychotherapist, John Tsiantis. I was in the second wave of international therapists brought over by Tsiantis. For preparation I went to speak to the late Professor Izzy Kolvin, who made the helpful comment, "Think shit". When I got to the beautiful island I was asked if I wanted a tour of it. I refrained, knowing I had a rite of passage to make in managing the sight and smell of the wards.

There was the archetypal, strangely familiar and yet unbearable scene. The huge, cold, shit-smelling wards and the old iron beds and naked, smeared patients huddled together. This was what I had prepared for. I strode across the ward to one particular over-crowded bed and said in Greek, "Hello. I am Valerie Sinason from England." And I held out my hand. Contrary to warnings I did not wear gloves.

From amongst the mass of human pain, a man with Down's syndrome untwisted himself and shook my hand.

And then I walked out of the ward and into the clean staffroom where I scrubbed and scrubbed my hands and felt both sick and ready for work.

A year later, I saw the young man in the first group home for learning disabled people in Athens. He opened the door when I had rung the bell. We recognized each other but had no shared verbal language. We shook hands in an ordinary way. He was smartly dressed and took me on a tour of the house pointing to furniture. I was then given an interpreter to hold a group and think about the feelings they had about leaving others behind in such terrible conditions. The young man looked at me and said, "I remember you. You shook my hand on Leros."

Two different handshakes and such different continents of meaning. Where touch is not allowed, all that variation in meaning cannot be "grasped".

### Ritual abuse and touch

Sarah had been ritually abused. She had left and lost her abusing family to come to the United Kingdom. A highly intelligent, successful professional, she was both delighted and shocked when she found she was pregnant by her loving partner.

"How can the baby live inside me? It is disgusting in there. Second-hand. Spoilt. Things in the wrong place. If walls can talk, surely the walls of my womb are covered with graffiti of horror. The baby will go mad just being there. Did I tell you? They shoved shit up my vagina. They packed me up inside with it. Said I was shit inside and outside as well as stuffing my mouth with it. I've washed and bleached and swum and showered and disinfected for years and years but that shit has got to be still inside me. Please. Hold me. Just hold me."

And I sat down beside her on the couch and held her. She cried and cried.

That was the only moment of touch in six years of once-weekly psychotherapy. Sarah gave birth to a lovely and loved baby.

In working with those who have been made to take part in activities that are socially seen as repellent (eating faeces, eating parts of human bodies, torture, incest) or those with profound multiple disabilities and malformations, we are getting close to enormous feelings of other-ness, alienation, and self-disgust.

## *Dissociative identity disorder*

Maureen was a successful lawyer in her mid-thirties who had friends who were psychotherapists. She had read a great deal about therapy before coming to an assessment. She had been ritually abused in childhood and was struggling with flashbacks, as well as periods of lost time. She specifically wanted a psychoanalytic treatment. Unlike most of the traumatized people I have met, she made clear she was quite happy to lie on the couch.

Only after a few months did it emerge that Maureen was not the only client. The sound of a crash in the distance followed by police and ambulance sirens triggered a change, and from my chair behind the couch I could see the elegant, normally very still, Maureen turn into a foetal ball. A thumb went into her mouth and little child-like gasps and sighs starting coming.

"That noise was very loud," I said.

"I'm fwightened," said a little voice.

I shifted on my chair. The figure froze.

"I'm sorry I frightened you moving," I said.

There was silence.

Stifled childlike sobs emerged.

I said I was Valerie and I knew Maureen. Did she know Maureen?

"Ye-es. No. I'm not supposed to say."

She cried again.

"Where's Meg? Meg looks after me. Where has she gone? Bad girl Mandy. Meg's gone away." She hit herself in the head and began a litany of self-hate.

I gently moved from behind the couch to a chair alongside.

"Hello," I said in a very soft voice.

"I am bad. You can't say hello to me."

"That's hard, being little and bad," I said.

"Can I hug you?" she asked.

"What is a hug?" I asked.

"It's this," she said putting her arms round me.

"It's saying hello with all of your hands and body."

"Hello," she said more brightly. "Can I play here?" And off the couch she went, picking up soft toys, all her movements like that of a very small child.

In the basket of toys was a baby doll. She picked it up and gave it a hug. In that moment she disappeared and Maureen reappeared, sitting in her smart work suit on the carpet with a baby doll in her hand.

"What the hell is this? I did not ask for primal therapy or some weird fringe stuff. I wanted psychoanalytic treatment. On the couch. Neutrality. No play. The whole works."

The self-hatred engendered by the abuse had made soft loving touching feelings dangerous. Here a verbal treatment had been specifically chosen as an important defence against feeling. Such work involves many complex ethical and technical issues.

## Bringing in a supplementary support body therapist

In running a clinic for those who have been deeply traumatized, I have had the freedom to make links with a range of other treatment modalities, including cranial osteopathy (John Silverstone), reflexology (Carole Mallard), and body therapy (Roz Carroll) and others who have been able to share in a process of damage limitation or even improvement.

At different moments in clinical work with patients suffering with pain from their torture I have, with great care, brought in a co-therapist for a few sessions who could offer cranial osteopathy, reflexology, psychodynamic body therapy—whatever the patient felt like trying. Consent for touch has been carefully established and is restricted to perceived non-sexual parts of the fully clothed body—such as hands, neck, head and shoulders, feet. With a few exceptions, where a patient was able to travel independently to the osteopath, for example, such work has taken place in my consulting room and in my presence. This will be written about in the future.

## Conclusion

Our personalities help to unconsciously choose the training we undertake. At a time when there are so many different psychotherapy trainings it is very important that we look into the reasons for the particular choice we made. It will automatically enhance one area of our thinking and understanding and wipe out another.

Words can hurt, eroticize, disgust, violate, confuse. They can also heal. Bodies can hurt, eroticize, disgust, violate, and confuse. They too can offer healing. All communications are double-edged, whether physical or mental or both. A word for some patients is a physical object. All communications have to be thought about carefully, and their transferential implications. However, the automatic ruling out of one mode of communications is a certainty that needs questioning.

# CHAPTER FIVE

# Can touching be relevant to understanding some patients in psychoanalysis?

*Pearl King*

E very therapist, whether they realize it or not, brings their background and requirements with themselves into the consulting room, whether they are a patient or a psychotherapist or a psychoanalyst. Whatever behaviours they were required to have, or whatever roles they had to fulfil as they grew up from childhood to adulthood, has affected the way they treat those with whom they live or work, and what they feel about them. Many people would see this as their cultural and psychological background, which they take for granted, "Because it happens to everyone, does it not?"

If they decide to apply for one of the training courses in psychoanalysis or psychotherapy, requiring a simultaneous psychoanalysis as part of their training experience, the ways in which they faced or avoided the restrictions or possibilities imposed on them by authority figures as they grew up will no doubt be aroused. Such training courses should involve the development of their understanding of themselves, of how they have reacted to, or behaved towards, other people that they were, or are, in a relationship with. This will, of course, have been unconsciously embellished by their past experiences and fears, by their personalities, and by their needs to be accepted and appreciated by colleagues and rivals.

However, there are other influences that may escape careful study and understanding in the course of an analytic experience, especially if the theory that their analyst follows belittles the role played by outside events or the context within which their patients grew up. I refer to the cultural ingredients of their behaviour, their assumptions about people, and the cultural context within which they grew up.

## Cultural setting and the handshake

When I was a student being trained to be a psychoanalyst by the Institute of Psychoanalysis in London, just after the end of the Second World War, there were a number of people of different nationalities in our group of students. As we listened to each other, trying to operate and understand our new role as psychoanalysts, we also became aware of how other factors were influencing the behaviour of our colleagues.

One evening we were listening to one of our male colleagues reporting a session with a young Cockney woman, whose therapist had an American accent. It was obvious to us that she could not always understand what he said to her, nor could he always follow her Cockney slang. Eventually it emerged that she was wondering why he always shook hands with her at the beginning and end of every session. It only gradually dawned on us that this student, with his American accent, was not in his usual cultural setting, where people would have taken his accent as normal speech. Furthermore, our thoughts turned to considering who was his training analyst. We remembered that she had come from Europe, where it was accepted as polite behaviour to shake hands with people who are important to you, or in a role with you, both on meeting and parting from each other. Although she had been in this country for at least twenty years, obviously, if she still continued shaking hands with her patients it must be very important to her or part of her cultural being. We students drew the conclusion that this must have been accepted by our American fellow student, and he had repeated the behaviour of his training analyst with his treatment of his patient, without having explored either its meaning within their analytic relationship or his patient's resentment at having this "strange behaviour" taken for granted.

Shortly after the Second World War, in 1949, when I was working for the Tavistock Institute of Human Relations, it was my job to help to arrange a European Conference of Public Health Nurses, which was to take place in Holland. As I had to travel from London to Holland, I arrived late for the meeting I had called to make plans for this conference. I found that most of them were already sitting around the table, reading the information that I had sent them from London. I apologized for my lateness and sat down, as I would have done in London. Shortly after this, a delegate from France arrived, but before sitting in her place and joining the group, she walked around the table and she shook hands with everyone in the room. I thought to myself, "That is what I should have done!" I then asked myself, "Why do they do it like that? What is the meaning of the handshake? What was conveyed to each person whose hand she gripped of past and present, and maybe of future, experiences together?"

It then came to my mind that I had arrived from Britain, a country that had not been invaded and taken over by a ruthless army, unlike many of my fellow delegates. Some had been virtual prisoners in their own country, maybe unable to trust anyone. Again I thought, "Do they have to touch each other before it is safe to trust themselves to relate to other members of this conference planning group?" They came from at least a dozen European countries, some of which had fought against each other during the war. Under the cover of helping to set up or revive public health services, which they all needed, it was relatively safe (emotionally) to let each other be in touch with the pain and anger of each other's thoughts, hopes, and tragedies, which did not have to be put into words but which could be held in their handshakes.

Now, as I write this over fifty years later, I am confronted with how out of touch I was then with my own cultural context. I had not picked up that they could well have been jealous of my having been protected from being invaded, even if I had been heavily bombed for much of the time. I would be seen as one of the many British, Americans, and Allies who came to Europe after the war to help them rebuild the shattered social structure of their and our continent. How hard it is when one is in a difficult and complicated situation to be aware of the pain of that situation, and yet to watch and monitor oneself in it, being aware of what it means to the other people who are sharing it with one.

Our relationships with patients start when we first contact them, often by a phone call during which a date for their first meeting with us emerges, accompanied by our address and how to reach it.

I remember Dr John Rickman saying that he would welcome a patient as he would welcome any genuine visitor into his house. I took this to mean that one should work from a culturally accepted baseline. Dr Paula Heimann agreed with this approach. Both would give a welcoming handshake, as I would also have done. The only other time when I shake the hands of my patients is after the last session before a long break in their analysis. It is a firm handshake, and in my mind I hope to convey that I am well and will look after myself while we are parted, because I know that my patients have to rely on me not to do anything that could endanger my being there to continue to work with them when they return for their next session. They often have a hard time looking after themselves over the time of the break or holiday. As I always open the door of my house to patients, I do not think that I always welcome them back with a handshake. The checking up on each other is passed to the act of seeing each other, which is better than shaking hands, which can be done without looking at each other. Their analyses can then continue. With the help of the patient's free associations these analytic partings and meetings were often fruitfully explored.

## Touching in the transference situation

In a book of papers by John Rickman, which I have recently compiled and edited, he writes,

> Psychoanalysis is the name given to a method of research and therapy discovered by Freud (1896c) based on a study of "free associations" in the "transference situation" and to the body of data and theories about the unconscious mind and its relation to behaviour which that method of research and therapy discloses. [Rickman, 1947, p. 71]

The transference situation he describes as an "instrument", e.g., like a microscope, which is needed to study small objects, or a telescope for distant objects. It is a social relationship (most clearly seen in the case of two persons) which permits the spontaneous appearance of repressed unconscious phantasies of the person analysed to crystallize in reference to the person, and his environment, who is analysing that individual's personality and social relationships and which gives access to his transference neurosis. Rickman continues,

> The therapeutic co-operation between two adults has superimposed on it all kinds of emotional cross-currents from the past of which the patient was consciously quite unaware, and of a strength and intensity which he could not believe possible. This past situation transferred to time present and dominating the physician–patient co-operation is the transference situation (Freud, 1912b). [Rickman, 1947, p. 74]

Now, is there any warning in what I have written above, based on John Rickman's description of psychoanalysis, which might indicate that it might be particularly inadvisable for analysts, of their own volition, to come into physical contact with their patient, or to touch them? It is important to remember that, while in English touch usually refers to physical contact, it can also refer to emotional contact. A patient might say to his analyst, "I was very touched by the way you helped me yesterday", if, for example, the patient had tripped and seriously hurt his ankle on leaving his analyst's consulting room, and his analyst had helped him to stand up, and had lent him a walking stick, so that he was not unable to support himself, and asked him if he would like to order a taxi or an ambulance.

The urgency of that current situation might well blur or hide from the analyst the fact that he and his patient had not been able to make a careful exploration of the transference situation, which might have revealed, to both patient and analyst, his real problem: that he had felt lonely and unloved when his mother went to hospital when his rather sickly younger brother was born, and that he felt that his needs were never noticed and no one helped him with his anger about how he felt.

John Rickman writes,

The treatment consists in disclosing to the patient the operation of these early and buried impulses and seeing them in their past and present setting; the art of the treatment lies in the maintenance of a quiet, interested, objective personal relationship throughout the storms and confusions of these transference phenomena; the science of the treatment, so to speak, lies in the employment of the simplest possible technical (theoretical) aids to the understanding of what is going on.

The data provided by following the free association rule and the transference phenomena are given some sort of order if it is assumed, and this is a basic assumption, that when any two ideas come together in temporal association there must be some common link or links of meaning. The patient's resistance frequently challenges this assumption; it is usually, if not invariably, a counterattack to cover a sore spot. [Rickman, 1947, p. 74]

Like everything that occurs in the transference situation, when touch occurs it can usefully be explored and thought about along the lines John Rickman describes. In the course of working in the transference situation, past wishes, fears and day dreams are evoked, involving loves and hates, hopes and terrors, past and future traumas, as analyst and patient shift their way through their developmental blockages. The work that I have been describing was from an adult neurotic patient, of the kind that Freud's theories and methods of work were evolved to guide our work with.

## Working with children and touching

I would like to conclude this chapter by discussing some of my experiences of touching a patient when I worked with a child patient under the supervision of Donald Winnicott. My patient was a boy of four years old who had been traumatized, as I was told, by seeing his two-year-old brother fall out of a window to his death.

This boy's main way of communicating his problems to me was by "acting" a situation that was in his mind, in which we were both to be involved, rather than by saying what came into his mind. He was a child who could not play until almost the end of our work together. While working with this child, I soon discovered that I had two main tasks, both of which involved touching him. These were to prevent my patient from hurting himself and to prevent him from hurting me. No way could I carry out these tasks without touching him.

He often started a session by announcing what we were going to do today. He would give a short summary of a situation and tell me what role I would have to act in his "vignette". "Today you are my mother and I am your baby; you will cover me up on the couch." After a while, he would get up and then I was the baby and he was mother (I gradually became "his" mother) and he covered me up and told me to sleep. I do not think that father came in for a long time.

Sometimes I had to carry him around, as he was a very small baby and could not walk. Sometimes I was given one role and then later the roles were reversed. One day, after I had had my hair set, he announced, "And today we will wash your hair!" "Not today," I said, "But instead we will wash my hands together." And he ran to the water, washing my hands and then his own hands, and enjoying splashing with the water.

While I was acting in these vignettes, I tried to put into words the anxieties and the pleasures and the fears that had been contained in these episodes or vignettes. One day he announced that today I would be his horse, and he told me to go on to all fours and he would ride me. Then perhaps I was a donkey. He tried to climb on to my back and then decided that I would give him a piggy-back. I thought to myself, "I wonder what Melanie Klein would do with this child?" I had attended her seminars on child analysis and I thought of her as sitting quietly in a chair all through a session.

Then one day he came out of the lavatory without his trousers on, and told me to pick him up and show his bottom to the different objects in the room, as if I was introducing him to them. This really had me confused, and I took this session to my supervision. When I came to describe my carrying him around the room, and introducing him and his bare bottom to the items in the room, Winnicott said, "He wants you to understand that sometimes he sees the world through his anus, and do you understand that? Can you share his point of view and see what he sees?" I said that this made sense to me, but I also thought that he wanted to know what I feel about the contents of his body and his mind. I said, "He may have fears that are too dangerous to talk about in case they become true."

It was shortly after this that he picked out one of the cupboards in the room and made it into a tube train like the one that brought him and his mother to his sessions with me. He was feeling very gloomy. He said to me, "I want you to lift me. I'll try to be as light as I can, but we are going in a lift." Then the lift in the corner of the room turned into a tube train, containing his mother and himself. He was in a great panic, and said, "You must push me out." Then he said, "The baby's been pushed out, the baby's gone, it's been electrocuted." So I said to him, "You know, I think that you're terrified that on your way here your mother's going to push you under the train and kill you." And he was very relieved and the session went on and ended peacefully.

I had been able to do all the work with this child, fitting in with his language requirements, until he could turn me into his angry and terrifying version of his mother, who could kill him, as he believed she had killed his younger brother, by not looking after him. I think that all the contact and touching that was part of these vignettes were also a context to protect him while we worked our way to this session, and the analyst/mother whom he feared wanted to kill him, and saved him from his nightmares becoming real.

Looking back on the work that I did with this patient fifty years ago, it seems to me that touching means many different things according to the context within which it takes place, and this also depends on the theoretical background of the therapist and the developmental stage that the patient has reached. I think that the vignettes that the child and I helped to create together did become a protected area within which changes in his inner world could take place and become understood as safe to acknowledge and share with me. Could some process like this be relevant to understanding other patients?

# CHAPTER SIX

# Bearing witness to an abused patient's physical injuries

*Graeme Galton*

I n my work as a psychoanalytic psychotherapist there has only been one occasion when I have had deliberate physical contact with a patient—except for sometimes shaking hands—and it is this occasion that I explore in this chapter. I will try to make clear some of the issues that I think were relevant to the situation with this patient, a woman who had suffered severe and ongoing sexual, physical, and psychological abuse when she was a child and adolescent and whose body still carried serious injuries from these experiences. I will also try to assess the effect of this touching on our subsequent work together.

## Clinical material

The patient, whom I shall call Anne, was a woman in her thirties who had suffered severe sexual, physical, and psychological abuse through-out her childhood and adolescence. She was five years old when her great-uncle raped her and subsequently introduced her to a gang of paedophiles. These abusers were highly organized and subjected Anne to terrifying rituals and horrific torture, with the result that for many years Anne was in a chronically dissociative state as the only way to get through this sustained trauma. Her dissociation enabled her to survive, but it also ensured that she remained compliant and that she would not be believed if she reported the abuse. Such was the extent of her dissociation that Anne did not feel the pain of the torture, nor did she tell her parents what was being done to her. Anne's parents did not recognize for themselves that the abuse was occurring. This may sound surprising, but the reasons are complex and not directly relevant to this discussion, so I will not present them here. The abuse continued until Anne was nineteen years old.

When I began seeing her, Anne was no longer dissociative and could recall everything that had been done to her by her abusers. Considering her extraordinary suffering, she had made remarkable progress, but she still had considerable emotional and psychological difficulties and her life was severely restricted. Anne's short term and long term memory was severely impaired, although she could remember the abuse itself and all the details of her extensive dealings with the police and medical profession. She could also now feel the pain in her body that she had not felt at the time of her abuse. She bore extensive physical injuries that had not received medical treatment when they occurred. A number of bones had been deliberately broken by her abusers and had not been properly set, including her toes and other bones in her feet, her knee, her ribs, her fingers, her collarbone, her nose, and her cheekbone. She had disc damage in her back and her jaw was dislocated. Damage to her hip affected her posture and a tear in her left thigh muscle made walking painful. Anne had suffered considerable neurological damage, with no sensation in her facial skin, limited muscle control of her face, and double vision in one eye. Her pelvic floor muscle was severely damaged, she had no bladder control and had no sensation in her front or back passage. Three times in her early adolescence her abusers had made her pregnant and then performed damaging abortions.

Anne spent much of the time in her early sessions with me describing the injuries she had sustained from her abusers. Indeed, an important part of establishing our work together was for me to bear witness to her traumatic experiences. She had faced considerable disbelief from the police, and from some members of the medical profession, and the injuries to her body were the evidence she offered to demonstrate the truth of her account. We were working face to face and issues around her damaged body were central to our work.

In one session with me, Anne was telling me about her recent visit to a new physiotherapist. In describing this encounter, she focused on the look of absolute horror on the young physiotherapist's face when she saw Anne's body. My patient was deeply affected by the physiotherapist's horrified expression. As she described this experience, mentioning in particular the physiotherapist's eyes, what came to my mind was Winnicott's (1967b) concept of the baby seeing herself reflected in her mother's eyes. It was as if Anne had seen herself reflected in the eyes of this young woman and had been appalled by what she saw. I encouraged her to say a bit more about how she felt when she saw the physiotherapist's expression and she could say only that it had made her feel sad. I was very touched by the image of this scene and by her sadness. Despite the physiotherapist's initial shock, she had been kind and sensitive and had begun a course of physiotherapy aimed at improving Anne's muscle tone and posture.

Later in the same session, Anne was describing to me an act of abuse she had experienced when she was nine years old. On this occasion, one of her abusers had driven a sewing needle deep into her knee and left it there. Anne had been dissociative and had not felt any pain, and the needle had been lodged so deeply that it was not visible. Remarkably, she had still been able to walk. Because she felt no pain and had no memory of the incident, the needle remained undetected in her knee until she was thirteen years old. One day at school she was jumping down some steps and she felt her knee crack, followed by severe pain. This time she did receive proper medical attention and the doctors were amazed when X-rays revealed the presence of the needle. She required three operations to remove the needle and repair the damage to her knee, including skin grafts. Anne explained to me how the surgeons had pulled fatty tissue from the sides of her knee to pad the damaged area at the front in order to minimize adhesions between the scar tissue and the bone. The doctors had said the effect would be temporary and sadly it was. Sitting across from me, she was wearing trousers and had been pointing to her knee as she was talking. She then felt her knee again and said to me, "You can feel it. Go on, see how it feels."

I sat there, surprised and unsure how to respond. As a psychoanalytic psychotherapist, I do not touch my patients and I usually shake hands only at the beginning or end of a period of work, and only then if a patient initiates it. Anne was watching me closely and I knew that I had only a few seconds to decide on my response to her request. I wanted time to think, time to discuss it with my supervisor, time to understand the real communication in this request. I felt I had no time because a significant pause in my response would itself be an important communication to Anne.

I was tempted to ask Anne what it would mean to her if I felt her damaged knee—but to do that would have felt as if I was avoiding something for my sake, not hers. I wondered whether to respond first to the manifest content of her request by explaining gently and compassionately that it was important for us to work with words in our sessions together, with no physical contact, and to try to express our thoughts and feelings verbally. But the image of the horrified physiotherapist was fresh in my mind and I believed Anne would interpret any refusal—or any hesitation—however sensitively and eloquently expressed, as a communication that I found her body too horrifying even to feel her knee through her trousers in order to "see how it feels". With these conflicting thoughts flashing through my mind in a matter of heartbeats, I reached forward, briefly felt the front of her knee and said, "I think you really want me to know exactly how your knee feels."

I hoped Anne would experience my touch as benign and thoughtful. She smiled and then went on to talk about something else. I do not know what she talked about because for the next few minutes my mind was completely absorbed in reviewing my decision. I was consulting my internal supervisor, wondering whether I had just committed a serious violation of therapeutic boundaries that would have dire consequences for Anne's therapy, or whether I had acted appropriately in the circumstances and provided a positive maternal mirror. I was later very much aware that by not tracking Anne's narrative immediately following my touch, I lost one important opportunity to check out my decision.

In considering my countertransference, I am aware that in Anne's sessions I was often very conscious of my own body in a visceral sense. Although I was not anxious, I was sometimes conscious of my breathing and heartbeat. I could feel the blood in my veins, and when I moved I was aware of my muscles attached to my bones. It was as if my own body was announcing its functionality, as if in defensive reassurance when Anne talked of her own body's lack of functionality. I had been experiencing this bodily sensation while Anne was describing her damaged knee.

## Discussion

What had I done to provoke the invitation to touch? I did not find Anne's body horrifying or disgusting and I am aware that I did wish to find a way to make this clear to her, but I felt no impulse to soothe her or offer safety by touching her. I do not believe that I was acting out my own anxiety at my helplessness in the face of the horrific injuries that had been inflicted on Anne. One line of psycho-analytic argument would perhaps say that I was in identification with the patient's need for reassurance and that, by alleviating her anxiety, I achieved a palliative effect that was unlikely to lead to psychic change (e.g., Klein, 1957). However, it seems to me that at this time Anne felt sad rather than anxious, and that she neither sought nor received reassurance from me.

I did not feel that our relationship was sexualized, but I did not know whether perhaps for Anne her knee was an erogenous area— or even a fetish. I was very conscious that I was a male therapist alone with a severely abused female patient, and that my first responsibility was to protect us both from potentially abusive expe-riences. I felt placed in an ethically difficult situation where my own sure safety lay in following the classical principle of abstinence. At the same time, I felt that if I refused to feel her knee it would be abusive and traumatic for Anne, and damaging for the therapy. I definitely did feel a strong impulse to be a "better mother" than the physiotherapist, not in order to avoid Anne's intense feelings, but to offer a positive maternal mirror, as a prerequisite for healthy ego development. In this respect, these circumstances were quite differ-ent from those faced by Patrick Casement (1982) when he decided not to be a "better mother" and did not allow his patient the possi-bility of holding his hand. He judged that the interests of that particular analysis required the patient to re-experience a childhood trauma without the possibility of physical contact with him. Further, he had needed to demonstrate to her that he could bear her neediness and her most intense feelings generated by his refusal.

I did feel that I was in a position where it was difficult to say no. Perhaps, to some extent, Anne was unconsciously placing me in the helpless position in which the abusers had placed her, a position where it was impossible to say no. There may be some truth in this, and part of her may have been in identification with the aggressor in this way. It is also possible that the sustained impingement she had experienced had given her a confused sense of her body's boundaries. However, Anne had never touched me in any way, not even offering to shake hands. Her recognition in this session that touch required invitation suggested that she did indeed have a clear sense of her own bodily boundaries.

Orbach (2003a,b) suggests that a person's body is a set of possibilities that is first co-created between an infant and her or his primary attachment figures. Later, other significant figures in a person's life participate in the ongoing co-creation of her or his body. Orbach borrows from Winnicott's famous phrase, "there is no such thing as a baby, there are only instances of maternal care", and she suggests, ". . . there is . . . *no such thing as a body, there is only a body in relationship with another body*" (Orbach, 2003a, p. 11, original italics).

It is evident that Anne and the physiotherapist had co-created a body that was horrifying. Even before the physiotherapy treatment had commenced, they both hated that body. It seems possible that, as a result of this alone, the physiotherapy had little chance of making any improvement. This was confirmed several weeks later when Anne reported that the physiotherapy was making no difference. She said they were wasting their time, that they were "flogging a dead horse". Her use of this particular phrase seems to carry significant meaning in this context: her hated body had become the lifeless carcass of an animal. Furthermore, this dead beast was being cruelly whipped, echoing the earlier abuse in her life. What sort of body had been co-created between Anne and her abusers? Her complex relationship with her body perhaps included her body as receptacle, as the hated object of abuse.

If Anne's embodiment had been shaped by the abusive touch of others, then perhaps the physiotherapist's gaze, and subsequent touch, had also served to shape her body. The physiotherapist's conscious desire to improve Anne's posture was at odds with the unconscious communication between them, which had shaped an altogether different and horrifying body in that first exchange of looks. That co-created body was fixed in their relationship and the physiotherapist's subsequent touch had no power to change it.

When Anne asked me to feel her knee, perhaps she was repeating the scene with the physiotherapist, and countless other scenes where the relationship had created a hated body. Perhaps there was, to some extent, an unconscious wish to master this abusive experience by repeating it. However, I believe there was a simultaneous and more powerful wish to engage in a reparative experience by reshaping her body in the therapeutic relationship. I believe this was the primary unconscious communication from the patient and it was this that guided my decision to feel her knee.

Laplanche (1970) suggests that trauma can persist as an alien entity that lives on in the survivor, likening it to a spine living under the skin. There is an obvious and gruesome parallel here with the damaging sewing needle that had been lodged in Anne's knee, under her skin, as an actual spiny foreign object embodying the traumas she had suffered. Somehow there is a cross-over here between the symbolic and the concrete. One of the reasons often given for not touching a psychoanalytic patient is the belief that action hinders a patient's symbolic functioning, which needs to be developed by using words. But with Anne's traumatic sequelae in concrete form, perhaps we needed to acknowledge the literal before we could move to the symbolic.

The moment when Anne asked me to feel her knee might be regarded as what Stern et al. (1998) would call a "now moment". They suggest that such moments represent the non-linear progress of the psychotherapy, which proceeds sometimes in unexpected directions by leaps, not increments. Now moments arise unexpectedly and require from the therapist a response that is too specific and personal to be a known technical manoeuvre. There is often a strong sense that the course of the psychotherapy will be determined by the outcome of such a moment. In particular, now moments may occur when some aspect of the traditional therapeutic frame has been broken, or risks being broken, or should be broken. They suggest that if successfully negotiated, such moments can result in a "moment of meeting". They make an important distinction between two kinds of understanding in psychotherapy: explicit, declarative knowledge and implicit, procedural knowledge. They suggest that "just as an interpretation is the therapeutic event that rearranges the patient's conscious declarative knowledge, . . . a 'moment of meeting' is the event that rearranges *implicit relational knowing* for patient and analyst alike" (Stern et al., 1998, p. 906, original italics).

This can create new organizations in the therapeutic relationship and in the patient's implicit procedural knowledge; that is, her way of being with others. Anne's severe memory problems indicated that her retention of explicit, declarative knowledge was limited, although it was clear to me that she did remember some of what was said in the sessions. None the less, it was possible that her retention of implicit procedural knowledge was less affected by her memory problems and therefore offered the better chance of lasting therapeutic effect. It may have been helpful to Anne if I had drawn attention to the parallel between her request for me to feel her knee and her encounter with the physiotherapist.

Casement (2000) rejects the use of touch as a deliberate technique, but states that he feels at ease ". . . with the possibility of touch with *some* patients in *some* circumstances" (p. 163, original talics]. He believes that what determines whether it is right or not right cannot be found in any rule or prescription, but within the context of the particular patient and the particular therapist. Hale and Sinason (1994) believe that working with patients who have suffered ritual abuse, like Anne, can occasionally require the psychoanalytic psychotherapist to touch the patient. Sometimes physical contact is necessary either to protect the patient from self-injury or to provide mental containment. Touch was especially important when patients described their involvement in particularly disgusting practices because, ". . . physical contact assured them that they were still human and capable of human contact . . ." (Hale & Sinason, 1994, p. 279).

Alongside the issue of my touching Anne's knee, is the question of what interpretation, out of all the interpretive possibilities that could be derived from the myriad understandings outlined above, would have been the most appropriate. Jody Messler Davies (2002) reminds us that the therapeutic choice is not which interpretation is right and which is wrong, but, rather, which comment out of all the possible comments is the most important one for the patient to hear at that particular moment of time and opportunity. Davies believes this judgement needs to take into account which self states of the analyst and patient occupy that particular interpretive moment. At that time, much of my work with Anne had consisted of bearing witness to her abuse and her injuries—which had not been acknowledged by most of the professionals whom she had encountered—and I note that she used the words, "See how it feels". And, as I felt her knee, I replied, "I think you really want me to know exactly how your knee feels." Although much of my conscious awareness in that moment of touching centred on providing a positive maternal mirror in contrast to the physiotherapist's horrified gaze, perhaps it was primarily the witness in me that spoke and primarily the disbelieved survivor in her that heard and received my interpretation.

Anne's treatment proceeded well following the session described above, and in several years of subsequent therapy there was no further physical contact between us. We explored the event in the sessions following, and over time I was able to express several of the interpretative comments that I have outlined above. Despite her memory difficulties, she continued to remember the event clearly for the duration of the therapy and would refer back to it from time to time. Although I regard the rightness or wrongness of my decision as a still open question, I believe Anne regarded that single instance of physical contact as evidence of my capacity to acknowledge her injuries, to be in touch with some of her pain, and to work with her to create a less hated body.

# CHAPTER SEVEN

# Between touches

*Nicola Diamond*

## Introduction

This chapter examines two general but fundamental themes relating to touch and psychoanalysis. The first section of this chapter explores why touch is prohibited in psychoanalysis and what this suggests about the hidden meanings given to touch. The second section asks: what is the nature of touch and what is its potential as a communicative sense? In addressing such basic issues as the meaning of touch, its nature and potential, this chapter raises fundamental and foundational concerns that have relevance for psychoanalysis and for the clinical situation as such.

The purpose of this exploration is to identify preconceived prejudices concerning touch and to open up the space to consider touch afresh as a form of communication. In order to move away from reductionism in a definition of touch, the emphasis will be on the multi-faceted nature of touch, the way touch can be subtle, nuanced, and have the capacity for discrimination and multiple meanings.

The ability to emotionally touch another and to feel the skin surface as affectively sentient will be seen to involve an open sense of the experience of difference, otherness, and relationship. Touch is about a relationship with the other; touch can be considered a form of thinking, an affective "know-how" tied to emotional memory; and touch operates in a way analogous to the function of language.

The experience of touch will depend on the particular developmental and interpersonal historical trajectory of an individual. There are some people who fail to develop a discriminate and relational experience of touch. Certain kinds of autism are viewed in this light. The relational impairment of the sense of touch shows up more fully what is required in the usual experience of touch.

The third section of this chapter considers touch in the context of the symptoms and issues unique to the therapeutic situation. The purpose is not to advocate the use of touch in the analytic relationship, or to condemn the use of touch in unique and carefully considered situations, but rather to open up an understanding of touch and to help us engage in its significance and complexity.


## Section one

### Psychoanalysis and the touch taboo

Since the birth of the "talking cure" there has been a taboo on touch. What are the assumptions about the nature of touch that underlie and give rise to such a taboo?

Freud moved away from physical treatments, towards hypnosis, and then away from hypnosis and towards the "pressure technique". The "pressure technique" involved touching his patient's forehead while she or he lay supine, to facilitate associations. This technique was then abandoned for pure free association. Certainly, in this concrete form, we can see that the actual changes in Freud's technique reflect the move away from touch and the institution of the taboo.

There was the case of Breuer and Anna O, where her desire for Breuer led to a phantom pregnancy and the implied consummation, which terrified Breuer. The fact that such an implication could be experienced as an accusation, and the potential ruin of Breuer's reputation could have resulted, was something to be defended against. No doubt this situation contributed to the inhibition of touch, in order to preserve the male physician's reputation.

Related to this is the idea that touch can bring about the breakdown of boundaries, that the transgression of physical boundaries will *necessarily* lead to the collapse of emotional boundaries and also of meaning and intention. I emphasize "necessarily" because the assumption is that touch has to be prohibited because there is something about the nature of touch that leads to the collapse of an emotional boundary and discriminate meaning. It is this necessity that leads to the enforcement of the taboo that is of interest.

One comparison that comes to mind is Lévi-Strauss's (1963) analysis of the necessity of the incest taboo for the birth of culture. Lévi-Strauss's argument is that incest would result in biological familial inbreeding and this would make it no longer necessary to breed with non-biologically related families. The cross-links and networks between families that results in an emergent community bound by social ties would not take place. In contrast, the incest taboo brings about a cross-fertilization and hence a definite social exchange between families not based on blood-ties, but a network of relations resulting in social bonds, a culture.

Of course, in the case of psychoanalysis there is no need to break blood-ties and the like, but I suggest there is a parallel between Lévi-Strauss's idea of the necessity of the incest taboo for a possibility of culture, and the idea of the touch taboo being necessary for culture in the consulting room. This, I would say, is an unsaid assumption that, if spoken, would go something like this: "touch breaks down discriminate boundaries and hence thinking and articulate sense, so it needs to be prohibited, in order for culture and symbol to exist". Whereas, according to Lévi-Strauss, the incest taboo gives rise to the possibility of culture, in a similar vein, the touch taboo in psychoanalysis makes possible the cultural space for the symbol.

What I am trying to get at here is that there are deeply ingrained prejudices about the way touch has been conceived, and that these beliefs about touch are so taken for granted that they are seen as givens and go unquestioned. I wish to make these implicit assumptions conscious and named, to name a prejudice to touch in traditional psychoanalysis.

Touch and thinking are conventionally viewed as antithetical. This goes as follows: "thinking is aligned to speech—the talking cure—and not to touch. Speech is linked to discerning thought, a key feature of the human species that brings us into the realm of culture and civilization. Touch is viewed as an immediate and basic primitive form of communication, more present and less discriminatory as a sense". We can say that the presence of touch is associated with an immediate failure of discriminatory sense, the difference between affection, erotic caress, or differential meaning immediately is elided with its introduction. There is the assumption that touch tends to annul the reflective space of the analytic encounter. A borderline relation to the symbol is readily evoked where symbolic equation automatically takes precedence as a dominant mode. In this model, touch can only be concrete in nature, rather than an act with a multitude of possible meanings.

### Psychoanalysis and "common sense": hierarchy of the senses

Where touch is given this more base status, there is an implicit hierarchy of the senses. In contrast to the immediacy of touch, vision is posited with a spatial relation of distance. Speech is further viewed as somewhat intangible—it evokes the non-presence of the object it represents in words and can open on to the symbol and thought. Speech is aligned with the capacity of nuanced and differentiated thinking.

This hierarchy is more fundamental than psychoanalysis. Psychoanalysis reflects in its particular way assumptions deeply engrained in cultural attitudes that derive from philosophy as well as other traditions that filter into every day thought and become popularized as part of what is regarded as common sense. (I am indebted here to the Marxist, Antonio Gramsci (1971), for his definition of common sense as the sum of social ideologies derived from a complex network of traditions of thought that become popularized and shared as a common ground in a given community.)

In the post-enlightenment era, the following prejudicial binary is assumed: touch is aligned with body, and body is rooted in its materiality, close to nature and animality. Thinking is not of body and is associated with the "higher-order" faculties, speech, thought, language, and culture. Thus, the presuppositions that are specifically articulated in psychoanalysis concerning the talking cure and the status of touch also reflect a wider trend that relates to a paradigm belonging to a cultural era.

In asking the question, "What are the hidden assumptions that lie behind, and have given rise to, the prohibition of touch in psychoanalysis?", we uncover a debased sense of the meaning of touch, which has been handed down from historical and philosophical traditions, creating a hierarchy of the senses that has been incorporated in popular ways of thinking and in turn has been articulated in specific ways within psychoanalysis.

## *Section two*

### *Touch and relation*

To abandon the prejudices in respect to touch opens a space to consider the phenomena of touch in a different way. Rather than a debased sense, touch can be considered crucial for a relation of body with world. In the novel *The English Patient*, we find a description of the character Almasy with his terrible burns and their aftermath, a man who has retained all sense organs except for that of touch. He is incapable of perceiving anything with his skin, non-existent except for a mouth, a vein in the arm, wolf-grey eyes. Benthien suggests that sensory information transmitted by touch is essential:

> Sensory-motoric tonus must be continuously maintained through external stimuli. . . . The loss of that tension results in the fragmentation of the self, of memory, and of social relationships. Here it becomes very clear that, in the final analysis, the skin ego is no visual image of the self (as psychoanalytic theory suggests) but instead a sensation ego that establishes and continuously sustains itself through tactile traces. [Benthien, 2002, p. 220]

Benthien notes that without the experience of touch a person's connection with others and a world slowly disintegrates, he literally loses touch. All he has left is disconnected internal phantoms that have lost contact with a world. Touch, from this perspective, is a crucial sense, vital for being in contact with an environment and others, providing the basis of a qualitative–differentiated experience.

The Latin verb *tangere*, like the French verb *toucher* and the English verb *to touch*, means "to put the hand or finger upon" or "to affect with feeling and emotion". For touch to be touching, it affects us and implies a relation with the other, touching and being touched, whether I feel my own body as an object—as another for myself—or touch another's body as other. A sense of difference and relationship is required for "the soul to feel the flesh, and the flesh to feel the chain" (Emily Brontë, *The Prisoner*).

Touch is a reflexive sense in the way it involves a self–other relation. Freud, in his initial discussion of narcissism, refers to primary narcissism and secondary narcissism, positing a primary auto-erotism where the subject touches itself, prior to the "entry" of the other. Secondary narcissism is installed at a later date, and only then there is an encounter with the other, and thereafter the relation with another becomes a definite part of the self-relation structure. However, as Laplanche and Pontalis (1973) point out, primary narcissism ". . . is no longer seen as a state independent of any inter-subjective relationship, but rather as the internalisation of a relationship" (p. 256). What this implies is that secondary narcissism is already under way for a primary narcissism, since to take one's own body as an object of cathexis is to already experience it as an object—as other for the self—thus already inferring a relationship. When we think about it, the newborn is touched and mirrored from the very beginning by others, and we could even go so far as to say that the others' touch is before the baby touches itself. Although this is a very concrete way of putting it, and there is a development of the baby's bodily experience that has to take place, it is the case that the auto-erotic, even when I touch myself, is already in some way fundamentally relational and this gets built into the structure of sensory experience.

To unpack this a little more, I am going to venture beyond psychoanalysis into phenomenology, where the experience and phenomena of touch have been described. Merleau-Ponty (1962) describes what he refers to as the touching–touched relation, where a person touches their right hand with their left hand (or vice versa). Merleau-Ponty is fascinated by the way touch evokes an ambiguous set-up where I am both subject and an object for myself, and can never be simultaneously one and both at the same time. When I touch my right hand with my left hand, my left hand is agent doing the touching and my right hand is the object being touched; I hop from one to the other, and cannot be one and other at the same moment; the sensation of touching and touched never wholly unites, something in body perception always miscarries at the last moment. Merleau-Ponty observes that instead ".... of perceiving the skin as a glove through which I can touch myself and find myself fully present in the contact I find I can touch myself only by escaping myself" (1962, p. 408).

Jacques Derrida (1976) comments, "In the experience of touching and being touched . . . the surface of my body as something external must begin by being exposed in a world . . . what is outside the sphere of my own has already entered this field of auto-affection". He continues, "The experience of touching–touched admits the world as a third party, the exteriority of space is irreducible here" (p. 165). The relational experience in touch is foregrounded here, otherness and exposure to the world being at the heart of auto-sensory being.

From the first, the other touches and we receive being touched, the experience of the skin is brought alive in being touched. Esther Bick (1968) suggests that a newborn placed on a mat, hands and limbs flaying in all directions, has no experience of a skin boundary. It is the touch of the other that brings about the cathexis of the skin, something Paul Federn (1953) also implies. Furthermore, Bick notes that it is the style of touch that gives the experience of the skin as a surface: continuous and contained or fragmented and unbounded, and so on. Didier Anzieu (1989) extends this thesis to show how the touch can be both literal and implied. Tactility is conveyed by mode of touch, but also by the co-terminus sonorous melody of voice, the significance of smell, the style of mirroring.

Bick, Federn, and Anzieu all note that touch plays a primary role in forming the experience of the skin, and that the other conveys nuance of feeling in style of touch and this is registered in early skin experience. Already there is an implied touch alongside the literal, and they go together. For example, the caretaker touches the infant, alongside flows the quality of voice and style in the touch that contributes to the subtle experience of the emotional sense.

### Procedural "know-how: and tactility

My purpose in drawing attention to style of touch and the constitution of early skin experience is to demonstrate that touch expresses subtle discriminations of feeling, and that the sense organs of touch in each one of us have a history that is rooted in the specific tactile relations with others. I want to stick to this level of the analysis and differ from Bick and Anzieu in this respect.

Whereas Bick and Anzieu move away from what they consider primitive touch and skin experience to the development of a mental–psychic image, I do not. This is because their move is part of the difficulty that I addressed earlier, which has to do with considering tactility as a more primitive order, in contrast to think-ing and the advent of the symbol, which is viewed as a higher order faculty that is not of brute materiality but of thought and mind. In contrast, I wish to stay with Benthien's point, considering the skin ego as rooted in sensation and tactile traces.

From the work of attachment, developmental psychology, and neuroscience studies, the so-called pre-verbal interaction between baby and caretaker is considered the basis of emotional communi-cation. Trevarthen (1993) notes that the basis of linguistic language is in the rhythmic–musical patterning of emotion that forms out of the interpersonal and sensory expression of feeling shared initially between baby and caretaker. In other words, we begin to move away from a linguistic definition of language, understanding the experience of language as based on a broader non-verbal basis.

Schore (1994) identifies the right hemisphere of the brain with affective and somatic function and as dominant for the first three years of life. He describes how the brain is directly stimulated and neurologically structured by the sensory pre-verbal interchange between caretaker and baby. Procedural memory is also associated with right brain function and has been described as storing sensory interpersonal experience as a form of "know-how", that is an unconscious (pre-reflective) affective–somatic knowledge that is activated and revivified in a doing way: for example, when we discover our movements and grace in dancing, or in the driving of a car, as we do it.

In respect to tactility, then, I suggest that there are in the context of a particular interpersonal historical situation subtle feelings of touch, discriminate and differentiated, remembered in being and feeling, touched and touching. Tactile sensory experience and bodily memory go together and are rooted in action. When one remembers a lost lover of the past, this is not a cognitive recall but a ry and feeling one. The caress is relived where the lover used to touch, and goose pimples appear on the arm and a shiver runs down the spine. The relived body memory as sensation is the particular way of being touched that no one has managed to capture since.

## Between touches

Touch functions analogous to a language, which need not be tied to a narrow linguistic definition.

In the film *Johnny Got his Gun*, there is a scene of a paralysed man with his nurse who, in an attempt to communicate with him, touches his skin, tracing the outline of letters that form words on the surface.

What we need to consider when exploring communication through bodily contact is how meaning and the differences between meanings are transmitted. It is all very well, as in the example above, to think of a literal tracing out of words on the skin surface, but how do these physical impressions actually convey sense? Furthermore, in communication through touch words do not have to be used.

To say that touch functions analogous to a language may not seem a radical statement, but in fact, within the debates that exist, it is. In cultural studies there are attempts to link the body with social inscription, but the formulations tend to be limited in conception to an actual form of writing on the skin. In this area the work can get stuck, exploring the skin tattoo or other stigmata. To consider bodily communication in terms of marks on the skin is thinking in very linguistic terms, with the metaphor of writing taken literally.

Although I would argue that touch could indeed be considered a style of writing, the literal transcription of the linguistic mode on to that of touch takes us up a blind alley. It would not get us any closer to understanding how significance is transmitted through touch. Helen Keller learned language via touch on her skin, not through the tracing of outlines of words and objects as such, but through developing an understanding of the *differences* between one kind of mark and another, a repertoire of small differences that eventually were built into patterns of sense.

Physical pressure upon the skin cannot, in fact, leave signifying marks. Likewise, it is not the electronic impulses impressed on the skin that enables blind people to receive messages in the form of Braille. The alphabet is not transmitted via electronic impulses *per se*, but rather by the rhythmic discontinuity, which enables a relation of pulses. These rhythmic modes form styles and patterns that convey specific meaning.

The physical mark is now replaced with a spacing, a certain absence of touch that already distances touch in proximity, which allows for a between in touch and in-between touches. Interestingly, in his paper, "Project for a scientific psychology", Freud (1950a) notes that the sense organs register stimuli via an appropriation of period, a temporal delay, a rhythmic dissonance.

Merleau-Ponty (1962) similarly describes a hiatus at the heart of the touching–touched relation, referred to as "an invisible hinge", an "untouched touch", that allows for a relation, for touch to be touching, for ". . . my life and the life of others to rock into one another" (p. 151). Without punctuation touch would be a continuity of presence, and there would be no differentiation. However, absences, the coming and going of the other (and with this the introduction of small differences), are part of life, of any spacing in the experience of interaction, and this happens from the very beginning of life (the coming and going of the primary caretaker).

Interaction implicitly signifies through little acts: mother gives baby her breast and later withdraws it. She touches soothingly, then stops. She goes out of the room and then returns. The ebbs and flows of feeling, and particular nuance of affect, are directly expressed in the touch and its absences. It is not so much a deprivation of touch but more a certain withdrawal within touch for touch to be touching, a certain non-presence in touch and of touch. In other words, it is not a matter of absolutes, no touch in contrast to the presence of touch, but rather the absence of touch, of separation, becomes part of the experience of touch as such. A play of absence in presence, allows for some differentiation and relation in the experience of touch.

As stated, touch with no punctuation would be a continuous presence, touch and skin as on a continuum. Certain cases of autism described by Frances Tustin (1981), where the experience of separation is annulled, have precisely such an impaired experience of touch. In contrast, the spacing, the gap, the absence of touch, the mini separations, permit a rhythmic discontinuity, the possibility of differences and relational patterns of touch to be set up, bringing forth discriminatory and nuanced meanings and sense.

Anzieu (1989) refers to the prohibition of touch, but his analysis moves to what he considers a different realm, the psyche, and it ultimately still operates within a dualism. I am re-working the argument to say something different, to show how a certain prohibition becomes part of touch itself; in the very structure of tactility at the heart of sensation, there is the punctuation of absence, difference as a spacing between, registered and experienced as touch. In our model, every process is grounded in neurophysiology: tactile receptors transmitting stimuli and brain processes inseparably and simultaneously at work, producing patterned sense data and the experience of touch.

Touch can be discriminating, subtle, express deep feeling, and multiple possible meanings. We noted a certain non-presence of touch in touch, the play of the presence and absence of touch, to allow for rhythmic dissonance and relations of difference to be set up between touches and perceived as the style of touch. In this space of mini separations, for touch to begin to be touching, a relation to the other is installed in one's own experience of touch. This is perceived in the sensory ambiguity of touching and being touched. The intersubjective relation, the other and world as third party having already entered the auto-affective relation, thus bringing the sense touch on to the map as a discriminatory and meaning-giving sense. Touch can be considered a form of language.

*Some are not open to the relational experience of touch*

In certain cases, touch is not experienced as relational and differentiated, the space in touch, a certain non-presence in touch for it to be touching, to affect and alter, is blocked. Frances Tustin (1972, 1981) describes the experience of touch in autism where, instead of the touching–touched relation, there is, in its place, the generation of autistic shapes and objects. These physical objects are used to assure absolute body presence and self-proximity withou    ˙ˉnce. An object may be grasped so tightly that a physical ind left on the palm. Tustin notes that this assures absolu† and presence, no space, gap, separation, distance is She goes on to describe that in autism there is no aw difference between touching and being touched, or of others and body space, these children walk into objects and people as if they did not perceive them.

Tustin argues for a psychogenetic autism, noting no physical impairment of the sensory apparatus, and identifies trauma in early separation from mother. The devastation of loss in cases of psychic fragility results in the autistic defence, which blocks an experience of separation, absence, distance. Opiate levels in the blood fail to fall, so the neurobiological basis for the separation distress response is not activated. Psychologically, the sense of the other as different and separate is avoided and annulled, which results in an impairment in the auto-affective relation and in an awareness of others. In such cases, the skin cannot feel the touch as "other" and differentiation within the experience of touch is foreclosed. Such a case of privation in touch, in fact, shows up all that is in fact required for touch to be touching in the "general" trajectory.

However, Tustin's ontogenetic account of psychogenic autism is disputed. For example, Trevarthen, Aitken, Papoudi, and Robarts (1996) argue that the root of this embodied intersubjective disturbance is an organic defect. None the less, all agree that there is a fundamental alteration, and indeed impairment, in intersubjective relatedness and experience.

## Touch and development

Every experience has a neurophysiological basis, even, of course, any act of thinking, and brain–body processes are inseparable. It is ludicrous to rarefy the brain, as its structure and function are absolutely tied up with complex bodily processes. The neuroscientist Jaak Panksepp (2003) emphasizes that the brain is not isolated in a vat, but is of a body that is in a world.

We know hormones are stimulated by touch, and there is clear evidence in animals both for the stimulation of genital activity and growth hormones. In humans there are failing to thrive syndromes that are to do with affective neglect. In attachment terms, proximity and touch are essential for bonding and the affective communication that goes with it. Biologically, touch plays a key role in bonding, establishing the relational tie and, developmentally, for specific modes of interaction. It is hypothesized that complete privation of touch in early development leads to long-term impairment in social and affective capacity to relate (cf. discussion of Romanian orphans in Schore, 1994).

Touch is a complex and sophisticated sense, and it is a non-sense to construe a general and value-laden hierarchy of the senses. Although in evolutionary terms touch and smell were the earliest senses, it is the case that sensory information is essential for the development of the cortex in the brain. The cortex is associated with abstract and long-term thinking, the acquired functions, and touch develops as a sense as it becomes integrated in the cortex.

What is important is how a sense is used, and the trajectory of its development is crucial. The argument has focused on relational development and charted the capacities in touch that emerge in the encounter with the world and other, the auto-affective experience and relations with others that result in a discriminatory and differentiated experience of touch. The constitution of the self–other relation is structured and formed via interaction with another affectively and neurobiologically.

## Section three

### Touch and the meaning of the symptom

Depending on the trajectory of touch in the context of its meaning(s) in the analysand's history and current attachment relations, touch as a sense will develop in different ways, have varying potentials, and take on styles of significance. It is important to be engaged in a historical reconstruction of the analysand's tactile attachment relations and meanings from the situation of the present context and the analytic relationship, including the analyst's personal relation to touch, so that countertransference experience can be reflected upon continuously.

Freud, in his paper "The uncanny" (1919h), wrote of the experience of *unheimlich*. *Unheimlich* has a number of meanings, relating to the experience of strangeness, estrangement, not being–feeling at home, and can turn into its opposite: *heimlich*, the familiar, homeliness, etc. Lurking at the heart of the most familiar can be the feeling of not being at home at the same time. What can be uncanny is the double-ganger: the doll that comes alive, the phenomena that reveals the paradox of being simultaneously a subject and an object, a sense of alterity in the experience of subjectivity. In touch there can be the experience of *unheimlich*, of feeling in an uncanny way like an object, of feeling a sense of not being quite oneself; too much of that feeling can lead to the experience of being invaded, supplanted, engulfed and so on. Feelings of being depersonalized, of, for example, feeling half-machine and half-human have, of course, been documented in schizoid states (Tausk, 1933). Didier Anzieu (1989) has documented many patients' experiences, such as the sensation of a shrinking skin or of extreme fluctuations of temperature. Or there can be the experience of a lack of feeling, a numbness that feels strange and discomforting.

As part of touch, there is the experience of being like an object, the sense of others lurking in the sensation of touch and there is the particularity of the touching–touched relation in the attachment context that develops the sense of touch and sense of selfhood. With these aspects of touch drawn to our attention, it is now possible to explore the experience of alterity (not being at home and a sense of otherness) and the experience of touch in its specificity. I worked with a boy who had been sexually abused and suffered a perverse relationship with his older brother (Diamond & Marrone, 2003).

The most distressing experience for my patient came in the form of sensory states, which he felt spontaneously and which expressed the brother's malignancy at the heart of his sensation. In his anus, the sensory re-invocation of touch was one of pleasure, extreme perturbation, sadness, and the pain like a razor knife splitting him open from within, likened to broken glass shattering. In this bodily memory of touch as sensation, my analysand experienced the impossible paradox of sensation and association that put him in a state of fragmentation, most intensely captured in the touch that felt like a knife fracturing his insides and splitting him apart. The malignant otherness of the brother that allowed no space, that appropriated, took over, supplanted, and destructively annihilated his younger brother's embodied self-experience, was expressed in his tactile sense.

In another case, a patient suffered the sensation of pins and needles in her extremities, particularly in her feet and ankles, although no neurological basis in an organic disorder could be identified. Despite the lack of organic grounds, my patient often feared some crippling disease that the doctors had failed to detect. These pins and needles, a fizzing sensation, were extremely uncomfortable and the sensation felt as if it was not owned, not part of the self, as if something alien was inside disrupting rights to inner calm. The fizzing, a kind of buzzing, meant my patient could never sit still, for if she did, the sensation would take over. When in a constant fidgety movement, the fizzing would only momentarily and partially disperse.

The history of this patient is one of precocious development on the one hand, having to stand on her own two feet too early, and on the other a prolonged enmeshed dependency on her mother for advice and recognition. From her account, her mother was frustrated with her own life and over-involved herself with her daughter's life choices. Her father had a serious hysterical and neurological condition, which led to physical collapse at the most inopportune moments, and this continued in the later years. My patient did not feel safe in her own body and could not trust it, self-sufficiency and little emotional resource resulting in pseudo-sufficiency with a great vacuum within.

The intrusive fizzing constantly reminded my patient that it was not safe to be in her own body; there was this alien sensation that could not be incorporated into the body schema and which reminded my patient of the threat of illness. The void filled with some menacing alien sensation, like an imposing mother that intervened in controlling and selfish ways that could not be integrated as an agent of self-care, or as part of the patient's sense of subjectivity and healthy initiative. Her father's displays of physical and emotional collapse and disintegration were now a threat felt from within the senses. This is more than an issue of identification. It is the very constitution of the destructive otherness of both parents expressed in the alien experience of the fizzing, but now a structure of sensory being. The relational trajectory of the formation of the self and the perturbations therein are manifested as bodily states.

Roz Carroll, a body psychotherapist who works with touch and has written about the implications of neuroscience for psychotherapy, states,

> Interest is increasingly focused on neurochemistry in the dynamic equation of psychological functions. This implicates the totality of

bodily processes interacting with brain structures to produce a radical "new anatomy", where all psychological functions, even specific ego functions, are conceived of as emergent properties of a complex "brain–mind–body". [Carroll, 2003, p. 195]

## Touch and issues arising in the therapeutic situation

There is no doubt that touch is important and can be evoked in the therapeutic relationship even when actual touch does not take place between the people in the room. One cannot overstress the importance of depth and breadth in understanding, profound sensitivity, and a subtle sense of touch that the analyst and analysand need to have built together to broach the analysand's experience. As with all good analysis, the understanding, experience, reflective emotional capacity and attunement of the analyst is crucial, and is a real acquired gift that no good training can guarantee.

Increasingly, in the consulting room, we are observing the greater incidence of dissociation, over and above denial. It can be very difficult to detect dissociation, since the split-off part is so unacknowledged that it will not be evidenced in ambiguity, fragility, or any other way that we could infer. There was a woman in treatment who came across as having the capacity to be thoughtful and reflective. The therapist touched the client on the shoulder while she cried, believing he was helping her out of her isolation and emotional deprivation. The client cried and cried; it seemed a great catharsis. She was profusely grateful and left. However, she abruptly stopped the treatment, sending angry messages by e-mail, telling her therapist how she had never liked him and found him useless, that she was so full of anger and frustration that she would make every effort to destroy his reputation and that she had good evidence of his sexual advances.

In such an instance, the intervention with touch was based on the most superficial understanding of the patient. There was no exploration through the relationship of the split-off, dissociated her personality, and the significance of touch in the context attachment history and present relationships and, in particular transference relation to the analyst. Dissociation can be the state to detect in people who have a "normopathic" towards others and life in general.

The erotic transference in the analytic encounter presents particular issues. Erotic intimacy can be a radical opening to the other, involving an active unconscious surrendering of self for the sake of other. In the case of touch, letting go of the touch-for-me to the being-touched-for-the-other, is a powerful affirmation of loss of self. This is profound, as the very sense of touch is related to otherness, and when erotic love is involved we are dealing with a fundamental alteration of being. If there is erotic transference, the power of the fantasy and idealization of the analyst render the use of touch inappropriate. The analyst cannot in fact be a lover, partner, or parent and so on, even if "corrective" therapy is part of the work.

If touch is to be broached, the explicit creation of an "as if" space for an enactment can be helpful. In group settings this can been done with the explicit knowledge that this is a recreation of a scene from the past as a re-enactment and working through as in psychodrama; the deliberate creation of the scene as a play about real experiences but not in fact being real life. It can also be said that group settings militate against the privacy of individual work, the fact of a witness outside the couple and a socially shared sense of reality. In individual analysis, I would say it is essential to create the space of the analytic third, as Ogden (1994) has described; of course, this is always subject to the shared intersubjective space of the couple and the reflective process therein.

## Conclusion

In this chapter I have questioned prejudices concerning the nature and meaning of touch found in psychoanalysis and in "common sense". As part of the analysis, I have questioned the assumption that it is only thought and the word where the capacity of the symbol and processing can happen, and I have attempted to show that touch is potentially open to relational meaning, a sense of otherness, and the auto-affective turn of a self–other relation. However, this knowledge is procedural, related to emotional memory and, as part of that, an interpersonal "know-how" that is rooted in an unconscious pre-reflective process.

Real emotional change is not achieved through conscious reflection, but through altering the procedural interpersonal sense.

Conscious awareness has a role, but it is limited; what brings about affective change is what happens to pre-reflective know-how. This procedural non-linguistic mode of knowing can be directly addressed to bring about emotional change, rather than going through the linguistic root, which is one step removed and can even, in some cases, be so dislocated and un-integrated (with procedural knowledge) that it leads us in to a dead end.

Furthermore, the potential in the experience of touch, the style of sensitivity and mode of discrimination and openness to multiple meanings, relates to the development of touch in the interpersonal setting, the attachment experience, and will vary accordingly. In extreme cases, the experience of touch remains underdeveloped and the potential of touch can fail to be actualized or is foreclosed. Therefore, it is essential that the clinician has a real understanding and sensitivity of the analysand's experience of touch and its meanings if touch is to be broached as a field of exploration. A co-creation of a re-construction/construction of the history and current attachment relations is crucial. It is also the case that ongoing experiences of affectionate and erotic touch are important to consider across the life cycle. It is not a matter of a reduction to early development, although significant, but of a retrospective understanding of the past from the situation of the present.

Finally, in respect to the use of touch, touch can, of course, be broached without direct contact between analyst and analysand. As we can see in the examples of symptoms and the experience of touch, we are often dealing with how touch lives on in bodily memory and re-evocation. The metaphor is lived as sensation; the experience of touch is both real and also already metaphorical, as it evokes the experience of differences and meaning.

It is not that touch is dumb, but that we have a legacy of debasing the sense, which has made us dumb about touch. As for the use of touch in therapy, there are no simple answers to this except to question our prejudices and to be open to continual discussion and debate to allow for complexity and to work towards greater clarity of understanding in order to deal with the specificity of clinical realities.

# CHAPTER EIGHT

# The presence of the body in psychotherapy

*Em Farrell*

> Not to have confidence in one's body is to lose confidence in one's self.
>
> (Simone de Beauvoir, 1949, *The Second Sex*)

I have been in a floatation tank only once. It was a large one, enough space for seven of us to float around gently, taken around and around by a current. There was a ceiling of dark night and stars, round blurs to me, as I am very short-sighted. I had no difficulty trusting the water to hold me up, but I did not like it. I missed my body and the endless communication I am in with it. I did not want to be just a mind.

I am certainly not just a mind in my practice as a psychotherapist. I wriggle and move my legs and sigh and itch and pick my nails sometimes, and almost fall asleep, and this is with people who sit opposite me. I have, of course, much more physical freedom when someone uses the couch. There is, of course, a parallel process. The woman who goes to the loo, takes off her shoes and tucks herself into the armchair, like a cat on to a warm lap: she shifts around to find just the right space in the chair while I wait and watch. There is a relationship, conscious and otherwise, that goes on between our two bodies in the room.

Writing about this makes me feel uneasy. When I was asked to contribute to this book I hesitated. I thought, "I do not have anything to say". I do not touch my patients and they do not touch me. This almost goes without saying. It is accepted in the psychoanalytic psychotherapy world that touch is out of bounds and out of order. Yet, when I thought further, I remembered touch had been a large part of my own first psychoanalytic psychotherapy treatment and that during that time I had practised as a massage therapist. So I have received and given a lot of touch, yet I have pushed it from my mind. This chapter gives me the opportunity to try to think about it. It is not easy.

There is the very thin young woman who, through ten years of therapy and three changes of consulting room, always complained about the chairs that I provided. None of them was comfortable; they were all designed to make people sore and keen to leave after fifty minutes. In fact, I chose them specifically to push people out after fifty minutes. I responded over the years, and my chairs are more comfortable now. She finished her therapy while sitting in a relatively comfortable chair. There is quite a large space between the chairs, which is what I am happy with. It is, I think, a wider space than I would make between friends, friends whom I would be more likely to spontaneously touch, hug, or tease. So this physical space gives me thinking space and creates a boundary, which implicitly keeps physical contact at bay.

When first training as a counsellor in Edinburgh over twenty years ago, as part of a group of volunteer counsellors for students, we played two very physical "trust" games. The first involved being blindfolded and led around a house you did not know by someone you did not know. You were in someone else's hands in a very literal way. The other game involved all of us trainees. We formed a circle, and one person was chosen to stand in the middle. They were then pushed this way and that quite gently until they lost their balance and fell back into the arms of someone in the circle. The aim was not to drop them and no one did. None of the counselling trainings I have taught or supervised in London would dream of doing such exercises. Sculpting, where a group is modelled by one student in terms of his view of the emotional relationships within the group, is the closest I have come to it. The trust games worked; they were a powerful way of creating trust and openness in a group of people who worked closely together with an often quite disturbed population—interestingly, on the telephone.

There have been many studies done on the power of touch. Stroking pets can bring down heart rate and blood pressure, as can a hand on the shoulder. *Candid Camera*, a once popular TV show, did a wonderful sketch where they had an actor leave a five-pound note in a telephone box. He would then ask the person who used the telephone after him, a member of the unsuspecting public, if they had found his money. All of those he very lightly touched on the arm returned his money. All the others kept it.

Here I am, apparently trying to convince you of the importance of touch. It is an odd thing to do, because I have no doubt as to its importance. Susie Orbach (2003a, p. 6) says, ". . . we seem to have lost the body *as body* and the body as having *a psychological and developmental history of its own*" (original italics). This seems to me a crucial point. I am not going to advocate bringing touch into psychodynamic or psychoanalytic psychotherapy, but I do want to get clinicians to think about the bodily needs of their patients, which might include touch, and the impact that the therapist's body can have on the patient and vice versa.

As a psychodynamic psychotherapist I rarely, if ever, use touch in my clinical practice. It has, however, played a major part in my own career in the world of therapy. In 1989 I set up The Elizabeth Gentle Centre, a specialist centre for eating disorders using a two-pronged approach of massage and cognitive behavioural therapy. Massage was an attempt to address directly the level of body hatred and self-loathing many women with eating disorders felt and to help establish a relationship of trust between us. This would create a space where it was possible to think together about their eating problems and what could be done in a practical way to help them with those problems. It was usually short-term work, with most women coming for twelve to fourteen sessions. Most of them suffered from bulimia and most of them went away symptom-free at the end of the time. An obvious subtext was an attempt to encourage physical acceptance of themselves, often in the face of pro-skinny messages from society and their families, as well as themselves. Here are some quotes from articles written when I set up the Centre:

Physical self-hatred can be so profound that it is only by touch that bulimics can begin to feel their bodies are accepted by others, and acceptable to themselves. [Farrell, 1989a]

In massage you feel a strong bond with the person giving it. If you have a good masseuse and your body is not handled as if it is obnoxious, the bad feelings you have about your body start to disappear. [Farrell, 1989b]

Every Friday, Jane B., who for years has indulged in episodes of frantic binge eating and then vomited to rid herself of the food, goes to see a therapist and receives a twenty-minute massage after her counselling session. The counselling helps her get a new perspective on her problem, she says, while the massage is slowly transforming the way she feels about her body . . . Jane B. remembers being "very scared" when she was given her first massage. "It was hard to have someone touching parts of me that I didn't want to touch myself," she admits. Now she actively looks forward to her sessions. [Hutton, 1989]

The mixture worked for many women. The boundary was very clear, both in terms of time and choice. No one had a massage unless they asked for it, and some just had a back massage through their clothes. During the time allotted to the massage, this would be spoken about. As I write this now I am aware of the complicated issues of intimacy, sensuality, and sexuality that were present all of the time. Dealing with them in a hands-on way was helpful and did set up a good therapeutic alliance where cognitive behavioural work could go ahead. When my own interest became more psychoanalytic, using massage became more problematic, as it skewed the transference in complicated ways. There was a group of women, approximately ten per cent, who did not leave, who did not improve, and who wanted more. Their problems seemed more difficult to budge; massage did not shift how they felt about their bodies and cognitive behavioural work did little to alter their relationship to food. For this group, the slow, thoughtful work of psychodynamic psychotherapy seemed to be best.

Jeanne Magagna, a specialist in eating disorders with children, told me recently that massage is a part of the programme offered at the Ellern Mede Centre for Eating Disorders in London, that it is very useful for anorectics, and they are able to take it in as a straightforwardly good experience. Indeed, in 1972, researchers writing in *Scientific American* stated,

> Current research suggests that some of the effects of malnutrition may be offset by programs of environmental stimulation or increased by environmental impoverishment . . . Tactile stimulation, physical contact with the environment, appears to be a food that is as vital for development as is any protein. [Rosenzweig, Bennett, & Diamond, 1972]

Likewise, a medical textbook of the time said, ". . . the deprivation of body touch, contact, and movement are the causes of a number of emotional disturbances which include depression and autistic behaviours, hyperactivity, sexual aberrations, drug abuse, violence and aggression" (Prescott, 1971).

Working primarily with eating disordered patients, as I did for five or so years, I want to use David Krueger's words about the 300 eating disordered patients whom he saw. "The body image of each patient is disrupted—blurred, distorted, indistinct, or incomplete" (Krueger, 1988, pp. 56–57). In practice, I think people with an uncertain body image are experienced by me in the countertransference as physically not being constant. The amount of space they take up seems to vary. There is often a sense of not knowing whom to expect from one day to another.

I am not advocating the use of touch in psychodynamic or psychoanalytic psychotherapy or counselling, but I am arguing for an acknowledgement of its importance in people's lives. Sex and sexuality has long been a topic in psychotherapy, whether it was the furore set off by Freud's acceptance of infant sexuality or the slow but steady acknowledgement of the presence of the erotic in the consulting room.

Forer (1969), in his paper, "The taboo against touching in psychotherapy", says the taboo can only

> . . . confirm that patient's own conviction that words are good and touch is always erotic or destructive and bad. Both therapist and client need to learn tolerance for their own excitement and realize that fantasies need not lead to action. Thus the therapist's non erotic touch may break through the client's defences and help him separate and tolerate the two kinds of experience. [Forer, 1969, p. 230]

However, it seems to me unhelpful to create too much of a split between good and bad touch. Just like words, touch can be experienced, understood, and given in very different ways. My point here is that words have power, too, and can be well used or badly used. The tone of voice and the words used can comfort, assuage pain, or do the opposite, just as touch can. There may indeed be a role for touch, but it seems to me that it is unlikely to be a very large one. But it does need thinking about.

Forer implies that psychoanalysts view touch as only destructive, erotic, and bad. It seems to me a matter of rules. When touch enters the consulting room, if it does, I think it often produces feelings of shame, failure, and transgression. This may, of course, be true, but not always. Thought out and thought through touch is a different matter. When I massaged patients it was often a very powerful emotional experience and yet remained within very clear parameters. I do not use massage in the work that I do any more, but I am aware of a hierarchical assumption within the psychoanalytic field that verbal containment and understanding is better than physical containment and understanding. This needs to be questioned. In a recent article in the *Journal of Contemporary Psychotherapy*, entitled "Touch in therapy: An effort to make the unknown known", by Bassya Pinson (2002), five psychoanalytically orientated psychotherapists write about touching their patients. They did so in response to the individual needs of the patients and their specific circumstances and the patients felt helped by it. It seems courageous to admit to touching patients in the psychoanalytic world. What is not needed is a therapist acting out within the therapy, whether physically or emotionally.

Touch was an integral part of my first long psychoanalytic psychotherapeutic treatment with a senior therapist from the London Centre for Psychotherapy, whom I think defines himself as a Kleinian. I had hurt my back and found it impossible to put on my coat at the end of my first session with him. He helped me. I remember thinking that nothing he said made me want to return, in contrast to the assessor I saw, but the helpful touch meant I was prepared to return. I was very depressed and regressed. I had therapy five days a week, and for a period of time, I do not remember how long, physical contact helped me survive very painful and very primitive physical feelings. Things are never straightforward and I am aware of, on the one hand, thinking I would have either broken down or left therapy if a hand to hold had not been available, but at the same time I think my regression was encouraged and words not used in the way that they might been to provide an alternative form of containment. The boundaries did become too blurred for us both, I think, which led to inappropriate acting out on my part in relation to my body, both within and outside of the therapy. Once this phase of my therapy was over, no physical contact took place except a final handshake the day I left.

Part of the reason I stopped using massage when I began to work more psychodynamically was that I could not see a way of working with the physical at the same time. My focus shifted. I became more interested in people's internal worlds and their phantasies. I wanted to create a space for reflection rather than directly accessing feelings through bodywork. Psychoanalytic psychotherapy relies on the assumption that the material that needs to be worked with will present itself. This may include psychosomatic symptoms and a desire for touch. Sometimes it may be appropriate and other times, as with interpretations, produce unexpected results. A male colleague told me about a female patient of his who missed two or three periods after he shook her hand. He shook her hand because his therapist had always shaken his at the beginning and end of each term.

I see people three times a week, and occasionally four, and although I have had people wanting to hold my hand, the urge has more often been to be inside me physically, to inhabit me, either in order to have my body and so disown their own, or to find a body where they can begin to find their own. I would, if I felt it was right, hold someone's hand in therapy, but the situation has never arisen; understanding and feeling have been enough so far. This is not to say that I might not enquire into, or think about, how much touch someone may or may not have in their life and get them to consider it. Susie Orbach (2003b, p. 20) says, ". . . I wonder what kind of disservice we do by *not* touching" (original italics). My own feeling is that generally people self-select, and that they come to see a psychodynamic psychotherapist not expecting touch, whereas people who go to a massage therapist do so because they want to be comforted, held, and contained in a physical way. It may, of course, be that people come to psychotherapy in the hope of avoiding dealing with their bodies and their experience of them and that is where I might want to surprise them.

Because I do a lot of work with body image, obesity, and bulimia, I allow my free-floating attention to include my experience of both the bodies in the room and how they may be reflecting each other, meeting each other or not, as the case may be. This is much more available when we are both sitting up. One common parallel physical process, which is not touching, but is a drawing close, is the unconscious body mirroring that often goes on, regardless of the gender or sexual orientation of the person I am seeing. What I notice is that I have my hand on one side of my cheek in a certain position and so does the person I am talking to. Later we have both moved and yet remained synchronized without any conscious intention. This awareness also makes me notice when it is not happening, or does not happen. One man I see, whose partner has a terminal illness, often gives me toothache in sessions. The physical mirroring above does not go on, and yet I end up with sore teeth. It was only after it had happened quite a few times that I realised it was connected to our work. He had had a great deal of dental work done, after not going to the dentist for years, and it seemed to be a projection of the rage and pain that he felt about his wife's illness for which there was no path of expression, and the physical and emotional cost that it took out of him.

Another example of the use of my body concerns a woman who uses the couch. Her father died when she was sixteen, and she has been unable to acknowledge either his presence in her life or his absence from it. I am always aware of the time of year when he died and, on this occasion, I found myself with a cough in her sessions. She has never been easy, and I thought it might have been an unconscious way of stopping her talking, or at least of stopping me listening. I assumed that if it was to do with me being run down, it would have happened with other people I saw. It did not. Yet when I saw her next, I once again got an impossible tickle in my throat. I tentatively wondered aloud about her father's symptoms. She said he had a nasty cough for the few weeks before he died.

It seems to me that more conscious and concrete acknowledgement of the body is needed in psychotherapy. I remember when an anorectic woman I had been working with for many years asked me how I experienced her physically. I surprised myself by deciding to respond. She knew I did not normally answer questions, and the question of her desire to be seen and to be able to move was hedged in all the time by her fear of both what she might do if she was seen, and her fear of how she might be seen. I said to her that she seemed quite lanky and a bit uncomfortable with her limbs as though she was not quite certain what direction they might go off in unbidden by her. The risk she took in asking the question and my ability to respond helped her to feel safer physically in the room. She no longer looked as though she was always waiting for an attack, which would come about because I had seen her.

It also allowed her focus to move from herself to me and my body. We had survived working together through a pregnancy (mine). She became fascinated by the transition between inner and outer. Separation and its difficulties had been a constant theme in our work together, and the focus of her fear shifted from an anxiety about how she or a baby would survive, to an interest in what happens to a mother's body during the process of the baby coming into the world through the birth canal. She could not believe my body had not been torn to shreds. Her fantasy of a baby coming out of a vagina was that it was not survivable for the mother, who would be physically blown apart by the baby's pushing his or her way into the world. Her own psychic arrival in the therapy had been emotionally violent, murderous, and desperate, and this thinking and working through of the physical aspects of it was to be our last phase of therapy. She was terrified that she had damaged me irreparably. She reminded me forcibly of Klein's belief that all knowledge comes through the experience of contact with the mother's body.

Touch never beckoned with any of the people I saw above. I did, and do, try to bear in mind the needs of the body as well as the mind, and the individual's access to physical closeness and touch and exercise needs to be thought about.

The beginning and end of sessions, and the beginning and end of therapy, are where the boundaries between therapy and the world of incidental touch and social communication come under the greatest strain. Obviously enough, the issues of boundaries and touch seem inseparable. I had a supervisee who was completing a short-term contract with her first male client and mentioned that, on leaving the last session, he said thank you, and gave her a kiss on each cheek. I was aware of my surprise and my supervisee's attempt to make it sound normal. On exploring it, she told me that her tutor at college (where she is doing an integrative training) had said clients often touch the counsellor at the end of the last session. Her work with the client had been full of potential sexual anxiety, which had been much reduced after being thought about and explored in supervision and in her own therapy. I was aware of how underground it had gone, and wondered if these unasked for (consciously) kisses were an expression of this. When I said this to her, she blushed and admitted that she had had an erotic dream about him the night before. She felt quite ashamed both of the dream and the kisses. I suspect that if her tutor had not told her that a hug or a kiss was a fairly common event at the completion of therapy, she would not have told me at all.

The physical needs to be allowed into the world of psychoanalytic psychotherapy. There are sometimes unthought through exceptions, like shaking hands at the beginning and end of terms, or at the beginning and end of treatment. I sometimes do the latter, although not always, if I sense the person does not want to be touched. Often in the last session a handshake is my way of expressing affection and an acknowledgement of both what has been and what lies ahead. I am aware that the more the ending is a choice on both sides, and comes about because the work that needed to be done has been done, the more touch is not needed even in the last session.

But I want to return to shame. My supervisee felt low-level shame. When I speak to people about having started off doing massage and counselling I realize I feel shame as though there was something intrinsically less valuable in working with the body than working as a psychodynamic psychotherapist as I now do.

My hunch is that the more at ease a psychotherapist is with his or her own body, and using it in the work, the less the issue of touch is likely to be problematic.

Marion Milner (1969, p. 42) says, "I was beginning to believe more and more that what I said was often less important than my body–mind state of being in sessions". She continues,

> I had myself worked through the concept of "body-attention", or "concentration of the body", as something which one does while

trying to paint from nature, a kind of deliberate filling out of one's whole body with one's consciousness, so that one perceived whatever one was trying to paint with a whole body-attention, not just with one's eyes or one's head. So now I gradually came to guess that this was something that there was a special need to achieve in my relation to Susan. It was also almost impossible, since she was adept at producing a state of tension in me, not only by the urgency of her demands for help, but also by her total angry rejection of any idea that was not completely formulated. [*ibid.*, p. 48]

It seems to me to be good practice to try to do what Marion Milner suggests. It is hard, but if after a difficult session with someone you find yourself anxious and worried, then consciously trying to relax is important. It allows you to take more in and be more flexible.

Someone I work with told me she always used to feel she went through people and yet she felt she had not gone through me, she had bounced back off me. I had held up. It reminded me of a woman who said before she had had a massage, "I don't believe I have any bones. If you punched me in the stomach your hand would just go on meeting flesh. I don't have a skeleton to support me." Both of these women, in different ways, seem to be shouting out about the importance of being psychically and physically pressed against another in order to know about their own limits. It seems to me most women and many men are still in quite a muddle about their own relationship to their body, their sexuality and to food.

It may be that choosing to be a psychotherapist is a way of trying to avoid your physical self in the consulting room. Just as our minds and our words are the objects of unconscious phantasy, projections, and so on, so too, I would argue, are our bodies and we may need to be more aware of this and make more use of it in our work with the people whom we see. To consider how we are viewed and physically experienced and compared to the person we are with, requires a level of physical awareness that is not often taught in trainings. I was talking with a woman recently who was enquiring about what it was like to be me physically; whether I hated my body as much as she did hers. I asked what she thought and she replied that she was not sure. Sometimes she thought I did like my body and other times that I did not. What she was sure of was that my size had remained constant throughout the time we had worked together and she thought that this suggested some sense that I could bear myself in a way she finds difficult.

Just as when first working in the transference it is easy to feel you are drawing attention to yourself, and it can feel uncomfortable, so, too, when you start to bring your body into the room by talking about it. It can feel intimate and dangerous and yet, I would say brings me closer to my patients than touch would. For our bodies are feeling and being acknowledged and thought about and bumping off each other all at the same time. Perhaps this is why some of the people I see move from couch to chair and back again so that different things about themselves and their interaction with me can be thought about and understood.

I do not want to slip into saying that I think what I am describing is better than touch. I do not. People have different needs at different times in their lives. For some, psychodynamic psychotherapy may never be appropriate. For others, bodywork may always be out of bounds. And then there are all the people who could benefit from both. Touch does need to be thought about, for the more we can understand why psychotherapists use it when they do, the less taboo considering and thinking about it will become. It goes hand in hand with psychotherapists acknowledging their own bodies and those of the people they work with.

# CHAPTER NINE

# The issue of physical contact in psychoanalytic work with children and adolescents

*Maria Emilia Pozzi*

I am going to approach this topic from the point of view of child psychotherapy, and this includes babies, young and older children, and adolescents, some of whom may present with learning and physical disabilities, aggressive behaviours and gross acting out, autism, psychosis, and generalized developmental delays.

I would like to start with a personal vignette regarding my own personal psychoanalytical experiences in different countries. The first one took place in Switzerland, in my adolescent years, and it centred on working over issues related with growing up, leaving my family of origin, finding my place in life, but also on deeply entrenched infantile layers of my unconscious. Owing to these latter states and needs, it was of paramount importance to me that my continental psychoanalyst shook my hand at the beginning of each session—four times a week for several years—as she met me at the door of her consulting room, and at the end, when she accompanied me back to the door. This she opened and closed behind me—a very different habit from what seems customary in England. The warm, physical contact did, indeed, nourish me and did no harm to me, nor avoided difficult and painful issues for me, including those of beginning and ending sessions. One may still wonder whether the physical holding of the hand of my first analyst may have taken away the opportunity, for example, to analyse why such concrete, physical contact was so important to me. It was not only a sign of friendly and loving care directed towards my wounded psyche, but also a sign that my more aggressive and unpleasant aspects had not turned my analyst against or away from me.

It had therefore been a shock when I met my first analyst in London, who at the end of our first encounter sat waiting for me to leave the consulting room, and never stood up or shook my hand until the very last session. Then I grasped my courage to initiate the handshake, and was met by what I remember feeling as a slightly embarrassed but responsive shake of hand.

Alex Holder, a Swiss psychoanalyst who trained in London, also had to come to terms with this cultural difference, which he writes about in his paper, "To touch or not to touch": "In some countries like Great Britain or the United States, it is unusual to shake hands after the first acquaintance. In others like Switzerland or Germany one usually shakes hands whenever one meets and separates" (Holder, 2000, p. 49). He describes his experience with his London training analyst who, after a few sessions, asked him to refrain from shaking hands. He felt hurt but came to accept this as a cultural difference and later adapted to this English habit, even with his own patients.

Holder also refers to how much non-verbal communication his English and North American colleagues miss by not shaking hands at the beginning and end of sessions. After exploring some of the anxieties such as those of "getting too close, . . . being seduced or being engulfed", he decides that "in spite of such possible disadvantages, it seems to me that the nonverbal messages contained in the handshake far outweigh these possible drawbacks" (ibid., p. 50).

Since my first analysis was in Switzerland, close to where I was born, I was again analysed when I came to England to train as a child psychotherapist. Therefore, I feel comfortable with either custom and tend to shake hands with those Italian patients who choose to do so. I am indeed aware of, and agree with, Holder's observations on how much is communicated by handshakes and how they change with the changes in the patients' states of mind, at different points in their therapy.

Another question regarding touching is whether to touch or not to touch under ordinary circumstances in psychoanalytic psychotherapy or psychoanalysis, since it is fairly well accepted that this type of treatment is mostly a verbal one. This focuses on the expression of freely associated verbal thoughts or silences on the part of the patient and on their understanding and interpretation by the analyst or therapist, as well as on the observation of bodily movements, actions, postures and non-verbal communication, at large. The question is, I believe, under which circumstances it is acceptable to break "the rule of abstinence", to introduce physical contact at a specific point in the treatment of a specific patient and in what form. Patrick Casement's (1982) well-known experience and the debate it created comes to mind. He had offered—and later withdrew the offer—to hold his female patient's hand at a particularly difficult and crucial point in her analysis. The offer had been perceived by her as a sign of his weakness and of his need for reassurance, which she indeed provided him with, as her dream revealed. Casement believes the real therapeutic effect that has a reparative function, and differs from the original trauma, takes place when the patient has "a chance to find someone able to bear the impact of her feelings about what she was remembering" and also "to be *there* for what she had been feeling at the time when her mother had failed to be there" (Casement, 2000, p. 175). It seems to me that this is the best holding and containing experience that a patient can hope for in treatment: a prerequisite for repairing old wounds.

Schlesinger and Appelbaum define *abstinence* in broad terms:

> The analyst should not attempt to placate, bribe, or exploit the patient. Neither should he collude in transference fantasies or try to provide anachronistically what the patient, in his unconscious fantasy, claims to be the missing experience that is responsible for his troubles. [Schlesinger & Appelbaum, 2000, p. 127]

This is an interesting perspective, which goes beyond sheer physical contact and includes more metaphorical ways of touching or colluding with the patient's mind.

I shall start by looking at this issue in relation to one adult patient treated by a colleague abroad. Then I will dip mostly into the world of child and adolescent patients and mention some vignettes and my reflections over the issue of touching in treatment, and the differences between working with children or with adults.

## Snippets from working with an adult patient

Colleague SK from New Zealand reports the following experience, which occurred in the sixth year of twice-a-week psychoanalytic psychotherapy with a female patient in her twenties. The material had indicated that her father had sexually abused her when she was a little girl. It was known for sure that she had been physically abused by him. The transference to the therapist was that of a combined object, in that she felt that the therapist could abuse her at any moment—as her father had probably done—and yet, like her real mother, the therapist was perceived as being unaware of what had gone on with the patient's father. In a session at this point the patient recalled being in the bedroom with her father, who took his pants down to show a huge erection. She then blanked out and could not recall anything any more. The therapist and his supervising analyst had come to believe that the patient had been sexually abused by her father and what the patient had recollected was indeed already an abuse. During this session the therapist had felt extremely sad in his countertransference, distraught and shocked that such a thing could be perpetrated by a father on a young child. He struggled against believing that it was true but had to accept the emotional truth communicated to him, that the abuse had really happened, even though a memory of physical penetration was never recaptured by the patient. The therapist struggled to contain his sadness at such an emotional awareness, and not to cry. At that point the patient asked, "Do you think that my father raped me?" "It sounds as if he might have," he replied, at which point she burst out crying uncontrollably. This allowed the therapist to feel free to let a tear out and no long fear that his emotional reaction might intrude into her emotions. The therapist recomposed himself before the patient did and she was still crying when the therapist felt a strong impulse to go over to her and comfort her by touching her on the shoulder with his hand. During one of the many discussions which followed this session, the patient said that when she had turned around and saw the therapist with tears in his eyes, she then knew that he believed her and also experienced the emotional truth that her father had raped her. She also said she wished the therapist had given her a cuddle as she needed to have a close contact with him at that moment. The therapist replied, "We did have close contact."

This is a very clear example where the therapist was able to have an intense emotional experience of the projective identification of something intolerable and unthinkable from the patient, i.e., that she had been sexually abused by her father when she was five years old. It was through the therapist's emotional receptivity and transformation into words of such an experience: "It sounds as if he might have", that an unbearable truth could be contained and the patient believed its reality and accepted it. Moreover, the strong impulse in the therapist to comfort the patient by touching her shoulder was not acted upon by him. The patient also felt a similar wish, which she could verbalize later. When the therapist replied to the patient's regret that he did not give her the physical contact she had wished for and said, "We did have close contact", this helped her to verbalize the powerful emotions flying between them. That was an invitation to give up on a wished-for type of physical contact and to make do with a more symbolic, but still real, type of emotional link between them.

For a patient who has been sexually abused, the issue of touch is particularly charged, although there is "good touch" and "bad touch" and an experience of healing, loving touch could be argued to be reparatory of a sexualized, perverse touch. Nevertheless, therapeutic abstinence seems to have borne fruit in the case of this colleague. The patient tolerated the frustration of her desire for physical comfort by her therapist, and yet was aware of the shared emotional experience that they both had. She was subsequently able to move on in her life and become the proud mother of a baby girl. She was also able to acknowledge that treatment had helped her to regain the happy childhood memories she had had prior to the abuse.

At the end of therapy, the patient chose to hug the therapist, who did not reject this gesture, and both said goodbye with tears in their eyes. The context of this physical contact, initiated by the patient and accepted by the therapist, was then very different and was part of expressing—in a safe way—both the closeness that had grown between them through the therapy and the sadness of parting. The patient was also able to say goodbye in the way she wanted to, without projecting her wish into her therapist.

### Some vignettes from working with children and adolescents

The issue of physical contact in the treatment of children is different, as child psychotherapists are inevitably met with the issue of physical contact, especially when at work with very young or very damaged children. Perhaps a basic rule—almost corresponding to that of "abstinence"—is that of not initiating physical contact with the child patient. I am reminded of the role of the observer in the observation of babies within their family context, according to the Esther Bick method (Bick, 1964; Briggs, 2002). There the observer does not initiate holding of the baby or contact with the toddler but is receptive and available if the baby is given to her or him to hold or if the toddler initiates an interaction or a game with the observer. The younger the child in therapy is, the more likely it is that the child will sooner or later initiate some physical contact with the therapist. Alex Holder (2000, p. 58) finds that "various forms of physical interaction between children and their therapists are commonplace but that they are usually initiated by the child rather than the therapist, . . . [or] initiated by the therapist . . . [as] a response to something coming from the child".

This leads me to some reflection on psychoanalytic "rules", which I believe are there to define the therapeutic setting, to foster treatment and to protect child patients and analysts equally. It is to protect child patients from having their infantile pre-oedipal and oedipal wishes and phantasies not just acted out in play—which is the norm with children—but acted out in the real relationship with the therapist or analyst, in collusion with such wishes. By this I refer to situations when the boundaries between playing, pretending, child and adult may be lost by the therapist or analyst. The latter is also safeguarded from the temptation of acting out similar unconscious wishes and drives by the definition of the setting. The added complication in the work with children is the generational difference between the child and the analyst or therapist, who is in a different position of authority, power and responsibility *vis-à-vis* the child patient. The generational boundary is a reality factor in child and adolescent treatments; therefore it is even more paramount that unconscious phantasies are not fulfilled in the therapeutic relationship.

There are different types of therapies that use the body as a tool for psycho–physical healing, but I believe that the scope of psychoanalytic psychotherapy is that of increasing awareness of one's own mind and body reactions and functioning by means of words: the "talking cure". Sometimes it can be of great benefit with adult patients to combine a talking therapy with a more physically-based therapy. Often interesting results and a speedier emotional awareness can result from the complementarities and yet differences of such approaches. Equally, we find therapies with children where a more physical approach is used and the therapist is encouraged to express feelings and also physical contact with the child, if needed (Hughes, 2005).

I have been trained, in a traditional way, to practise psychoanalytic psychotherapy with children, adolescents, and later with adults, and I am fairly settled with following the rule of abstinence, especially with my adult patients. When I have assessed and seen adult patients from my own country—patients who may have been very new to this type of treatment—they have somehow conveyed to me an unspoken uneasiness at what must have been perceived by them as a stifled or cold demeanour on my part. Not only had they expected me to shake hands, which I indeed did, but may have wanted something more friendly and physical than just smiles and welcoming words. Perhaps they expected a touch on their arm or a slight pat on their shoulder and possibly that I took their coat, like fellow travellers meeting in a foreign land.

To return to practice with children, the younger the child, the more immediate physical needs and wishes are brought to the therapy and it is not uncommon that, for example, in order to facilitate the child–mother separation in the waiting room, the therapist not only accepts, but also actively initiates, taking the child's hand if needed. When treating severely damaged children, such as those presenting an autistic, psychotic condition or disability, it is not uncommon for the child to want to sit on the therapist's lap, to look into the therapist's nostrils, ears, mouth, etc. This happened to me as I treated a five-year-old girl who presented autistic traits when she was first referred. I used to put into words her concrete curiosity about me and my inside, her intrusive desire to be inside my orifices, to see what was there in them and to be inside them and my body, standing—in the transference—for the maternal body. In her attempt to be back inside the mother/therapist's body, this child expressed her regressive wish for a placental state, away from the terrors and impingements of being born and separated physically from the mother and terrified by the outside world.

Winnicott (1963), in referring to the treatment of psychotic or borderline patients, accepts that occasionally holding must take a physical form, just like a child with an earache who needs more than just soothing words. An evocative account of being analysed by Winnicott and held physically by him, as well as psychologically, when her psychotic and mad parts took grip of her, can be read in Margaret Little's personal record of her analysis (Little, 1985, pp. 31 and 38). He used to hold her hand at such distressing times, and also convinced her to go into hospital, and drove her there, to make sure she did not commit suicide during one holiday interruption. She was never damaged nor spared by all that, but was greatly helped and inspired, both personally and professionally by those eight years of analysis with him.

Holder (2000) considers different aspects of the child's need to give physical expression to wishes and phantasies that may require physical contact with the therapist. It can be a casual contact with very young children, which occurs while playing; in very disturbed ones it can be the only way to communicate with the therapist; the therapist, at times, needs to set limits to excessively aggressive or erotized physical interactions. However, with children as well as with adults, there is a "trend toward greater verbal expression" (Holder, 2000, p. 61), and the channelling of negative transference into more symbolic forms of expression, as in the case of the very regressed little girl treated and described by him. She eventually worked through her negative transference and penis envy, and could write a story about "How Mr Holder was a poo" (Holder, 2005, p. 120), and draw pictures, too.

I am thinking of my work with eleven-year-old Johnny, who had Asperger's syndrome, when he entered a phase in his treatment of acting uncharacteristically aggressively with me. He had been meek

and cut off from his feelings and from having much of a relationship with me, which had not stopped me from reaching him
through a modified technique (Pozzi, 2003). Then he began to be
more related, to the point of trying to kick me in response to some
comment of mine. He was wearing heavy boots. He was clearly
showing me how he experienced the contact with me at that time:
like a kick in the shins. After my unsuccessful interpretations and
verbalizations of his demeanour and angry feelings and anxieties, I
decided to set a practical limit by asking him to remove his boots.
He ignored that, so I warned him that I would have to remove them
if he continued to ignore my request. Still no reply, so I moved
closer to him and began to hold his ankle to take the first boot off.
"I do not like to be hit and hurt", I said to him. He then turned
against me, threatening to do me for assault if I touched him. I was
stunned by the violence of his perception of my action aimed at
disarming or disempowering him. His earlier attack on me was
projected into me and Johnny now expected a magnified reaction,
i.e., a retaliatory assault on my part.

Younger children may feel contained, albeit in a restricted way,
by the therapist removing their shoes at times of violent acting-
outs. However, Johnny did not, and he interpreted my physical
contact of holding his ankle in order to remove his boot as threatening and rendering him powerless, undefended, and as a retaliatory action on my part. I could not use other tools, such as stopping
the session, as he came unaccompanied and could easily get into
trouble or get lost in the street—as had happened more than once—
had I stopped his sessions earlier.

This experience with this boy taught me a lesson in caution; I
have learnt to always let a patient know that I will have to inform
his or her parents if I have to hold or touch them. Many of our child
patients have been actually physically and/or sexually abused and
assaulted by their carers, those entrusted adults who are supposed
to respect them. In today's climate, this is posing an increasing risk
to the therapist and we are beginning to hear of cases where alle-
gations—later proved to be false—of abusing and assaulting children have been made against much-trusted colleagues.

Here follows a very different vignette, as twelve-year-old Larry
was a severely physically handicapped young boy, wheelchair-
bound and extremely limited in his movements, apart from his

upper limbs and hands. He suffered from an unknown form of progressive paralysis, similar to but not quite, cerebral palsy. His speech was very impaired but just about understandable with much effort on both his and the listener's part. He used to be wheeled into the room, a medical one, where I saw him year after year for once a week psychotherapy. His escort usually left to go for lunch nearby, therefore I could not rely on her in case of need. I had to be more active with him than I usually am with patients, due to his severe motility limits. For example, I had to open his box, where pens, paper, glue, and scissors were kept, when he indicated that he wanted to use them. I had to take the paper out of his folder and take the lid off the chosen felt-tip pen.

I also struggled to differentiate, as we began therapy, between what he could really not do and what he pretended or believed that he could not do. It took some time to disentangle the real handicap from the secondary handicap (Sinason, 1992) and this became an ongoing topic in this long psychotherapy. In the first year, he had started asking me to lift him up in his wheelchair to move him to a more comfortable position, or to lift his leg as he was in pain. I did it, at first, without thinking, but soon felt uneasy and began to be in a dilemma. This became an excruciatingly difficult situation at first, since I knew from the referrer that he had been sexually abused by a male family member. He was also entering adolescence and had, from our first encounter in the waiting room, shown a keen liking of me. When we first met, it was like "love at first sight", as he beamed at me with a radiant smile and I, too, was struck and touched by his loving, friendly, and attractive facial expression. We knew we took to each other instantly, and this was despite my earlier anxieties about his physical appearance and my possible reaction to it.

I was particularly aware of the delicacy of the issue of touching him physically. I was also aware of his physical pain and feared acting cruelly had I not tried to lift him up to alleviate his suffering. I was in a no-win predicament: either I was like the sadistic foster father who was found to have hit him, or I was like the seductive family member who had abused Larry sexually. Had I agreed to move, and therefore touch, parts of his body, would he have had a phantasy that he had seduced me into doing something he liked, i.e., to touch his body? In the transference situation, a reversal would have then occurred: my professional and personal bound-aries would have been interfered with, just as Larry's physical and sexual boundaries had been infringed upon in the past. This would have recreated a seduction situation, but with Larry in charge this time. Meanwhile, I would have been placed in the position of the powerless, abused and confused child. I decided to verbalize this conflict in simple terms such as, "I'm not sure if you really need me to move your leg or your back or if you just like me to touch you!" In response to this verbalization of this dilemma, he looked at me with half a smile in his eyes, as if I had caught him red-handed. He burst into laughter and it became clear to me that he had tried it on. I then realized that I had touched on a rather tricky side of him. He agreed that he just wanted me to touch him.

With time I learnt to distinguish between his tricky side, which wanted me to touch him, and his genuine pain and need for help. The dilemma between cruelty and seduction, two equally disturb-ing options, was clarified by understanding my countertransference and by interpretation. I felt freer and freer in deciphering whether to hold and lift his leg—in order to lift his back two people were needed so he no longer asked for that—or just interpret his request according to the meaning in each different context.

How I learned to understand whether Larry was in genuine pain or was having me on was a matter of time and of getting to know him better and better. Larry would resort to tricky manoeu-vres in therapy, hoping to get sympathy and comfort from me, whenever he went through a difficult experience in either his exter-nal life or in therapy. This happened when his beloved foster mother gave him up for unresolved issues of personal matters with the Social Services Department; or when his committed social worker moved to a different department and stopped working with him; or when long breaks in therapy approached. At such moments of fragility of the external or internal establishment, Larry gave up his struggle and tested me, possibly to see if I, too, gave up my pro-fessional stance and resorted to, or indulged in, touching/moving his legs or feet to offer him some relief. I often also spoke of his body and his heart, too, aching when he was sad or distressed about people leaving. On those occasions he seemed to want not only my understanding presence, but also my physical contact with him, and this I said to him.

I wonder whether, when a child has such a severely damaged and aching body, words have a more limited effect and sometimes touch can produce the effect of a much-needed painkiller—which, indeed, he had to take a lot of prior to his back operation. The body took a paramount focus in his life, therefore it can be understandable how much physical touch was requested by him.

To be sure, he "won over" my analytic stance when he had to undergo a severe spinal operation and was in hospital for several months. I decided that I would visit him weekly, after initial disruption, in order to keep some link with him. He was very pleased to see me and was desperate to hold my hand, which I decided to let him do for a short while, as I sat by his hospital bed. I said that he was keen to somehow be allowed to break our therapy rules and hold my hand. I said this was indeed a special situation, there in hospital with many people coming and going busily, with distractions, and children in need calling the nurses and grabbing my attention away from Larry, which he did indeed notice. Therefore I did let him hold my hand for a short while, as it became an imperative for me that I did not reject this request of his. Larry was very impaired and had to tolerate huge frustrations, therefore to allow him to hold my hand gave him some sense of power and pleasure, which I had no heart to withhold. Whether that was a mistaken decision, technically speaking, I cannot comment, but I could not detect any repercussions after therapy was resumed again as normal once he left hospital and went back to his ordinary life.

Larry was a straightforward patient to treat—I often said he was the healthiest of all my patients ever—and he soon learnt my ways of translating into the transference what he said to me or drew on paper. His seductive tricks were soon to be easily uncovered, as he would give me a knowing smile, when I asked if he really needed me to move his legs or feet because he was in pain or because he liked it, i.e., for pleasure reasons. If he was in real pain, I was soon able to know that I had to move his leg or foot. His legs also trembled and shook the wheelchair badly if they slipped off the resting bar. If appropriate, I did interpret this shaking in the session context, as well as move his limbs to restore stillness. This happened more often when, after six years of therapy we began to discuss and plan an ending, also in view of his approaching eighteenth birthday. The ending was indeed an event that shook him to the core of his being, as I had been one of the most reliable professionals—and probably one of the most reliable people—in his life, so that I came to be part of it. It felt to me, and probably to him, as if we had to meet forever. I have to admit that he was for me the most difficult patient to end therapy with. He shook me to my deepest depths and tested my psychological handicap regarding the issue of ending.

Child and adolescent psychotherapists and analysts are not just transference figures, especially since we are now treating very disturbed, deprived, delayed, and handicapped children, who have missed out on many ordinary phases of their emotional and physical development. We are also "new developmental objects" as Anne Hurry (1998) puts it so eloquently. She writes, "Today, with growing recognition of the developmental element in all analyses, such parameters are becoming recognized as mutative elements . . ., and the term 'developmental therapy' is now also applied to work with adults" (*ibid.*, p. 38). She acknowledges a debt to the following analysts: Anna Freud, for having established a developmental help for children with developmental deficits or distortions; Hans Loewald, who proposed that the analyst was also a "new object" and the analysis implied new ways of being and relating; Veikko Tähkä, who "distinguishes three strands in the patient's use of the analyst: as *Contemporary object*, as *Past (transference) object*, and as *New (developmental) object*" (*ibid.*, p. 44) and this difference provides a "corrective emotional experience" for the patient. Hurry suggests that the analyst needs to "be prepared to move between the developmental/relational stance and the interpretative, as Anna Freud described" (*ibid.*, p. 71).

Therefore I believe that, by carefully drawing the line between what could have been bad, seductive, sexualized touch and caring, friendly, helpful touching, Larry was helped to apprehend the difference and to have a new and different experience of touching and of myself as a trustable adult, when I allowed him to hold my hand in hospital. I was touched by Alex Holder's sensitive solution, when he offered his very distressed adult patient the chance to hold his hand, which he had placed at the end of the couch, next to his patient's head, in case she needed it (Holder, 2000, p. 48). This offer on the analyst's part was enough in itself to contain the distress and anxiety in his patient, as she did not then need to actually hold his hand.

## Conclusion

In reflecting on the issue of physical contact or not, an essential difference between child, adolescent, and adult treatment is that, in treating an adult patient, there is usually an adult part that allies with the analyst and can eventually reflect and accept verbalization of the need for physical contact, as in the case of the colleague from New Zealand. Children are on a developmental path and their bodies and minds are more openly interconnected than later in life. Physical and psychological hurts and pleasures are more often inseparable, especially with younger children. Therefore to forbid, avoid, and interrupt certain types of physical contacts with them is likely to be experienced by the child as confusing, inappropriate, misleading, and rejecting. I remember that in the treatment of my under-five training patient, I was particularly inhibited, to begin with, in playing actively and even in responding to ordinary child-like requests for interactions. My supervisor pointed out to me that, in my paralysed demeanour, I was acting out my patient's projection of a depressed, unresponsive internal object, and probably also the reality of having a depressed mother. I was staying stuck with it, until the supervision clarified what I was acting out.

I hope I have shared some of the thinking and the dilemmas regarding this issue of touching when working with young children and adolescents, as well as some of the differences when working with them compared with adults' work.

# CHAPTER TEN

# Strong adaptive perspectives on patient–therapist physical contact

*Robert Langs*

I n this chapter I offer an overview of the communicative or strong adaptive approach (SAA) (Langs, 2004a) to psychotherapy and psychoanalysis (terms I use interchangeably). I then present an assessment of the existing literature on the issue of physical contact between patients and their therapists taken from the vantage-point of the SAA. Because the SAA is a new and distinctive paradigm of psychoanalysis, its view of existing writings is highly critical. The chapter concludes with a presentation of the findings of the SAA in regard to touching in psychotherapy and with a series of recommendations as to how to best deal with this issue should it arise in a particular treatment situation.

## The strong adaptive approach and patients' material

The SAA has emerged and evolved on the basis of a clinically derived, distinctive way of listening to and formulating the meanings and implications of patients' material and therapists' interventions (Langs, 2004a). Critical to its clinical methodology is the use of an unconscious process of confirmation (or non-confirmation) that forms the basis for evaluating the validity of therapists' interventions and the theoretical constructs on which such interventions are made.

Developed by means of years of clinical trial and error, the following are the highlights of the clinical features of the SAA and the theoretical constructs that have emerged through, and have been supported by, its unconscious validating process.

In regard to patients' material in psychotherapy, there is a sharp distinction between narrative and non-narrative communications. Non-narrative expressions include discussions, opinionated comments, advice, intellectualizations, speculations, interpretations, general descriptions, and the like. Such material is relatively unempowered and only minimally related to the deep unconscious motives that determine and drive emotional adaptations and maladaptations. By and large, non-narrative communications are single-message expressions, with manifest meanings and their implications; they tend to be devoid of encoded meaning. They are conscious system communications (see below) and tend to serve non-meaning and defence far more than meaning and revelation.

Narrative expressions include dreams and stories of all kinds, fiction and non-fiction. They are the carriers of the power and drama of emotional life and they are deeply connected to the factors that drive emotional adaptations and their vicissitudes. Narratives are two-message communications that convey manifest contents and their implications, and in addition, carry disguised or encoded contents and meanings. Their primary function in psychotherapy is to express in disguised form patients' unconscious perceptions of triggering, emotionally-charged, external events which are, as a rule, constituted by their therapists' interventions. In this respect, they are communications that stem from the deep unconscious system (see below) and they tend to serve meaning and revelation, although they can at times be put to defensive use. In substance, however, narratives are the basic carriers of emotion-related meaning.

Patients' manifest and direct responses to and comments about their therapists and their interventions are of little or no value in determining the most basic effects of a therapist's efforts and in therapists' seeking guidelines for decisions about intervening, such as whether or not to touch a patient. This is the case because they arise from the highly defensive and often self-defeating conscious system of the emotion-processing mind (see below). Patients' narrative responses to interventions are an invaluable source of guidance for their psychotherapists. This is because they encode correctives and advisories that come from a very wise and healing deep unconscious wisdom subsystem. In essence, then, responsive, positively toned, displaced stories tend to confirm therapists' interventions, while those that are negatively toned are non-confirmatory.

The manner in which therapists' create and manage the ground rules of psychotherapy is fundamental to the healing process. In this regard, in establishing the rules that pertain to how patients are advised to communicate in their sessions, therapists need to advise their patients to follow *the fundamental rule of free association* and say whatever comes to mind. Because of the evolved, in-built and natural tendency of the conscious mind to communicate intellectually and defensively—i.e., to avoid or minimize narrative expressions—the fundamental rule should be supplemented with *the rule of guided association*. This entails advising patients to begin each session with a dream or a fictional story that they make up on the spot. This combination of communication-related ground rules serves to counter the natural defences of patients' conscious systems and to facilitate the expression of deeply meaningful narrative material.

It is well to divide modes of psychotherapy into intellectualized and narrative forms. Patients' manifest material—be it an intellectualization or the surface of a narrative—tend to allude to the meanings of, and their reactions to, events that take place either within or outside of the therapeutic situation—mainly the latter. In contrast, with the exception of major disasters, patients' encoded material pertains to the meanings of, and their reactions to, events and transactions that take place within the treatment situation. Encoded narrative themes centre and organize around the interventions of their therapists and especially deal with those interventions that are frame- or ground rule-related. These considerations suggest that patients may or may not allude manifestly to an incident that involves physical contact with their therapists, but they will consistently work over their unconscious perceptions of such incidents in their encoded narratives.

### The strong adaptive approach: theory and technique

The unconsciously validated insights gleaned from these principles of listening and formulating have led to the following theoretical constructs and principles of technique.

The clinical observations developed on the basis of the SAA are best organized and modelled by a much-revised version of Freud's topographic approach, with secondary structural considerations. The fundamental organizing principle of this topographic model lies with the distinction and differences between conscious and deep unconscious adaptive efforts—perceptions, processing endeavours, and communications.

There is a universal mental module—an organized collection of mental functions—that has been naturally selected and has evolved to adapt to emotionally-charged environmental impingements, primarily in the form of triggering traumatic events. This module is called *the emotion-processing mind*.

The emotion-processing mind has a distinctive system (which is, of course, brain-based, but entirely mental in nature) devoted to the reception and assignment of incoming information and meaning to its two processing systems. Operating mainly on the basis of an anxiety gradient, the system receives all inputs outside of awareness—unconsciously or subliminally—and sorts out the various layers and kinds of meanings that are inherent to a given event or communicative expression. This work is carried out by a *message analysing centre* (MAC) that assigns each communicative element for processing to one of the two operating systems of this mental module—conscious and deep unconscious. These assignments are mutually exclusive—impingements forwarded for conscious processing do not enter the deep unconscious system and vice versa. The entire operation is under the influence of genetic factors, among which death-related incidents have the greatest effect—death-related traumas tend to skew the MAC's assignments of information and meaning towards the deep unconscious system, rendering the conscious system less well informed.

The two operating systems of the emotion-processing mind—the conscious and deep unconscious systems—are distinguished by the presence or absence of awareness, or potential awareness, in their adaptive endeavours. With the exception of immediate threats of harm, the MAC forwards all overly-threatening perceptions and meanings of events to the deep unconscious system for adaptive processing. As a result, the conscious system fails to receive or register many critical emotionally-charged events and meanings. This defence is observed and thought of clinically as *conscious system denial and obliteration*, and it is the fundamental defence of the emotion-processing mind. Repression is a secondary defence that is directed against the memory of consciously registered events and meanings, and against the consciously accessible fantasies evoked by these events and meanings.

The basic adaptive-survival function of the emotion-processing mind is located in the MAC, which has evolved to protect the conscious system and mind from an overload of anxiety-provoking, potentially disruptive inputs that would interfere with conscious coping and endanger the individual. This protective device enhances immediate survival, but does so at the cost of the loss of considerable information and meaning. On this basis, the conscious system is a greatly impoverished system of the emotion-processing mind.

In clinical terms, then, the conscious system appears to be devoted primarily to defence, largely in the form of denial and obliteration. These basic defences are supplemented with a variety of secondary defences, such as repressing, misperceiving, deceiving, rationalizing, acting out, modifying rules, frames, and boundaries, and more. All in all, the conscious system—conscious thinking—is an ill-informed and unreliable source of information and meaning, and very untrustworthy in its perceptions and formulations. This untrustworthiness is reinforced by two additional findings that speak for the limitations of conscious system choices and decisions.

The first of these added factors in the impairment of conscious system functioning arises because the information and meanings that are processed by the deep unconscious system are unbearable to awareness. As a result, the conscious system has no direct access to these contents and their implications. Deep unconscious wisdom, which is eminently adaptive (see below), has little or no effect on conscious system operations and adaptations—a feature of the emotion-processing mind that entails an enormous loss of adaptive resources. In this sense, the emotion-processing mind has evolved to protect human life in a manner that appears to render the emotion-processing mind in a basically impaired manner.

The second feature of the emotion-processing mind that contributes to the problem inherent to conscious emotion-related adaptations is the finding that the conscious system is affected by inputs from the deep unconscious system of morality and ethics (see below). As a result, conscious thinking and consciously orchestrated behaviours are influenced by deep unconscious guilt and consequent needs for self-punishment and self-harm. Indeed, conscious choices and consciously orchestrated behaviours often are fundamentally directed against a person's best interests and are antithetical to sound healing.

Another critical feature of the conscious system is a relative absence of universal attitudes, morals, needs, preferences, opinions, and the like. As a result, conscious system values and thinking varies from one individual to the next, and a consensus on critical emotional issues is impossible to achieve.

Studies of the evolution of the emotion-processing mind indicate that the basic cause of its compromised design is the likelihood that the critical factor and determinant in the natural selection of the design of this mental module has been the human, language-based awareness of death and the need to deal with and defend against excesses of death anxiety (Langs, 1997, 2004a,b). Death and the anxieties that it evokes constitute the major environmental challenges and motivating factors in emotional life. This applies to both human creativity and human emotional dysfunctions. There are three forms of death anxiety (Langs, 2004a,b): *Predatory*—the fear caused by situations of potential or actual harm, which prompts the mobilization of resources; *Predator*—the fear of one's own death-as-revenge for having harmed others, which is based on conscious and deep unconscious guilt and needs for self-punishment; and *Existential*—the fear of the inevitability of personal demise, which evokes the use of denial in its many guises.

As is true of everyday life, the most crucial transactions in psychotherapy involve the status and management of its conditions—its rules, frames, and boundaries. There is an ideal, unconsciously validated, archetypal, universal set of ground rules for psychotherapy (Langs, 1998, 2004a). Adherence to these rules is inherently supportive, ego-enhancing, and healing for all concerned, but doing so also evokes entrapping existential death anxieties. Departures from these ideals universally are disruptive and harmful, but they do offer a measure of denial-based defence against secured frame, existential death anxieties. One of the basic ground rules of psychotherapy states that aside from a possible handshake at the beginning and end of a treatment experience, physical contact between patient and therapist is precluded.

The deep unconscious system of the emotion-processing mind is open to all manner of anxiety-provoking incoming information and meaning. It processes these inputs entirely outside of awareness and it communicates its unconscious perceptions, processing activities, and adaptive recommendations solely through encoded or disguised narratives—i.e., dreams and stories.

This system has three basic subsystems. The first is called *the deep unconscious wisdom subsystem* and it is an enormously knowledgeable adaptive processing system that has the earmarks of an inner god because its knowledge-base is so much more extensive than conscious knowledge, and it operates at all times in the service of a person's best interests. The values and adaptive preferences of this subsystem are universal, as seen, for example, in its unswerving support for, and validation of, the ideal, archetypal ground rules and boundaries of psychotherapy. The adaptive wisdom of the deep unconscious system can be accessed solely through a process known as *trigger decoding*. This entails undoing the disguises in a narrative communication by using as the decoding key the event (and the strongest meanings of that event) that has activated and been processed by the deep mind. This is the only known means of accessing deep unconscious wisdom and bringing into awareness so it can be used for conscious adaptations.

The deep unconscious system also houses *a subsystem of morality and ethics*. While conscious system morality varies across individuals and cultures, deep unconscious morality is based on a universal set of values, which, in psychotherapy, are reflected in how one accepts and manages its rules, frames, and boundaries. Thus, adherence to the ideal ground rules is unconsciously experienced as moral and ethical, while departures from these rules are unconsciously experienced as unethical and immoral. This deep unconscious subsystem not only sets standards of behaviour, it also enforces these standards. Unconsciously, it orchestrates rewards for ethical behaviours and punishments for ethical violations. The conscious mind will act and make choices under the influence of this subsystem's views of its behaviours.

The third subsystem of the deep unconscious mind is called *the deep unconscious fear of death system*. It is organized around existential death anxiety and is the prime motivator of the defensive and denial-based activities of the conscious system—i.e., it is a major influence on the MAC and its processing assignments. A large part of consciously orchestrated human behaviour and reasoning is unwittingly and unknowing affected by deep unconscious guilt and fears of death.

For patients in psychotherapy, the deep unconscious system is focused on their therapists' interventions, mainly those that pertain to managing the framework or ground rules of treatment. The ideal, unconsciously validated, universal frame includes a set time and frequency of sessions, a private and professional setting, and a single, appropriate fee. It also features total privacy and confidentiality, and the relative anonymity of the therapist with no deliberate self-revelations, directives, advice and the like. Unconsciously validated interventions include managing the ground rules towards their securement and the use of trigger-decoded interpretations also are part of this ideal frame. The fundamental rules of free and guided association belong here as well, and contact between patient and therapist is restricted to the time and place of sessions. Finally, as noted, aside from an elective initial handshake, physical contact between patient and therapist is precluded.

## A critique of conscious system thinking

The viewpoint of the strong adaptive approach (SAA) on the issue of physical contact between patients and therapists is based on the above propositions and considerations. To prepare us for the discussion that follows, the following aspects of the above presentation are especially pertinent to the points that I shall make.

The existing literature on touch in psychotherapy is a manifest content-surface implication or conscious system literature. It is a largely non-narrative literature that makes use mainly of intellectualizations or extracts direct meanings from manifest dreams in ways that do not include a consideration of their evocative triggers and the use of trigger decoding.

There is a series of critical features of the conscious systems of both patients and therapists that detrimentally affects this literature and its thinking. For one, there is the absence of conscious system universal values and viewpoints. There also is the related unfeasibility of achieving a conscious system consensus on emotionally critical matters. Another factor is the unconscious influence on conscious thinking and behaviours of existential and other forms of death anxiety and the human dread of dealing consciously with death-related imagery and issues, especially as they are activated in an ongoing therapeutic experience and emerge in narrative form. Also affecting this literature is the influence of deep unconscious guilt and needs for punishment on conscious system thinking and choices—frame-related and otherwise. Important, too, is the conscious system's extensive use of denial and obliteration, which greatly interferes with conscious clinical observing and reasoning. There is as well a conscious system preference for frame violations because they entail the use of denial-based defensiveness that defend against intensely dreaded existential death anxieties. The conscious mind also is unable to recognize its own defensive and self-defeating inclinations, and the flaws in its thinking. The conscious mind also has a basic need to avoid expressions of deep unconscious experience and wisdom, as seen in its avoidance of, or inattention to, narrative expressions, and its disinclination to engage in trigger decoding. There is, too, a conscious tendency to shut off encoded narrative expressions, especially when their underlying meanings become strikingly anxiety-provoking. This is a mathematically documented trend that was found in both patients and therapists (Langs, Badalamenti, & Thomson, 1996).

Overall, then, by virtue of its evolved design, the conscious system is an unreliable source of observations (which are defensively skewed), theory making, and preferences regarding issues of technique. This lack of dependability and proneness to unconsciously motivated defensiveness and error is reinforced by the fact that psychoanalysis is a qualitative science. It is well known that all such sciences are basically flawed in ways that they themselves are unprepared to envision. Conscious system psychoanalytic thinking in respect to the issue of touching in psychotherapy is, then, almost certain to be at best, clouded and at its worst, basically in error.

Summing up, then, as seen through the lens of the SAA, the attributes of the conscious system of the emotion-processing mind and of the manifest, direct, unencoded communications that arise from its province, indicate that this system and its pronouncements are quite uncertain and often may be untrue and misleading. On the manifest implications level, it is all but impossible to distinguish deeply valid from deeply invalid propositions and interventions. They are an insubstantial and treacherous basis for therapists' formulations and interventions, and for patients' responses to them. Unwittingly, they seldom address the best interests of either patients or therapists, and they speak more often for defence, denial, guilt, self-punishment, and harm than they do for unconsciously validatable insights and emotional healing. In general, when symptomatic relief is afforded to patients by a therapist's use of conscious system reasoning and intervening, the basis for these paradoxical results is not deep insight and working through. Instead, patients improve emotionally through unrecognized mechanisms such as therapists' unconscious sanctions of their denial-based defences, sanctioned acting out, inherently destructive but relief-giving frame violations, and patients' unconscious realizations that their therapists are more dysfunctional than they are—a process called *cure through nefarious comparison* (Langs, 1985).

Conscious system forms of psychotherapy often, although not always, may include an easily accessed and deciphered superficial unconscious dimension. Most often, the so-called unconscious aspects of patients' material lie with implications proposed by the therapist of which the patient is unaware. These interpretations are highly biased and theory driven and they do not obtain encoded, deep unconscious validation—as is true of almost all conscious system interventions.

Along different lines, as is true of all theories, conscious system theories implicitly direct the nature of clinical observation and evidence that a therapist makes use of in making formulations and in documenting a particular idea, theoretical revision, or clinical precept. The theory points to both what must be included and what is superfluous. Basically, then, a theory dictates what the observer–clinician sees and does not see—the range of his or her vision.

Seeing more than is shown through the lens of a given theory is especially difficult and arises more often through serendipity or unexpected inspiration than observation alone. This is a major reason why a theory—i.e., the adherents to a theory—cannot see its own flaws, errors, and blind spots. And this is especially true of theories that are founded on qualitative, sense impression data and lack a quantitative grounding. I hasten to add that the SAA has, however, been the source of this kind of quantification and lawfulness for psychoanalysis and psychotherapy, but its efforts have been ignored by a field that not only fails to appreciate such research findings, but seems motivated to ignore them for fear of having to confront the flaws in their most cherished ideas (Langs, 1996, 2004a).

While its use is subject to personal influences, reliable judgments are available solely through obtaining narrative associations from patients, identifying their evocative triggers, trigger decoding the deep unconscious perceptions and processing efforts of the deep unconscious system, offering a trigger-decoded interpretation—interpretive or frame securing—and listening to patient's encoded narrative response to the intervention for validating or non-validating imagery. The patient's deep unconscious wisdom system is remarkably wise when it come to valid, healing interventions—it is the best resource we have today for guidance regarding psychoanalytic theorizing and techniques.

## Some basic essentials

As for the field of observation that is essential for sound thinking regarding the issue of physical contact, the following omissions are characteristic of the existing literature and need to be included in case reports to allow for a fair evaluation of a given clinician position on this matter.

A detailed description of the framework of the psychotherapy— its rules, frames, and boundaries. This is essential because the question of patient–therapist physical contact is a ground rule issue and the possibility that a patient will request such contact is deeply affected by the conditions of the treatment. Thus, this request almost never arises in secured frames—i.e., in the context of a

psychotherapy structured with the ideal set of unconsciously validated ground rules. In contrast, request for touching is not uncommon in modified frames where one or more of the ideal ground
rules have not been invoked or have recently been modified or
violated. Requests of this kind are interactionally determined and
not simply a matter of inner or transference-based needs within the
patient—the tendency to hold the patient solely accountable for
these entreaties overlooks the adaptive and interactional aspects of
all such occurrences and the therapist's basic responsibility for
setting the stage for most of these interludes.

Similar considerations apply to therapists' responses to these
requests. They, too, are affected by the conditions of treatment, as
well as by past and recent frame-related experiences in their everyday lives and in their own psychotherapies. While therapists' (and
patients') handling of each of the individual ground rules is important, especially critical as factors in evoking patients' requests for
physical contact with their therapists are deviations in the nature of
the referral (e.g., prior personal contact with the therapist); therapists' failures to sustain their relative anonymity (e.g., personal
revelations and opinions); lack of total privacy for the office setting
(e.g., home–office settings); violations of the total confidentiality of
the therapy; and any recent, notable ground rule violation.

The antecedents of appeals for touch must be carefully noted
and documented, especially as they pertain to therapists' most
recent interventions. Both extended silences on the part of the
therapist (which may be appropriate or a reflection of a missed and
much-needed intervention) and his or her active comments and
behaviours (especially those that are frame violating) are among the
critical triggering interventions of therapists that unconsciously
may motivate patients to request this particular frame violation.
Indeed, touch is always unconsciously refuted and perceived as
seductive and harmful by both patient and therapist.

The case material, then, both before and after a patient's request
for physical contact, must be presented in great detail. While sum-
marizing is inevitable, the exchanges between patient and therapist
need to be presented in sufficient detail to allow the reader to independently assess the conscious and unconscious nature and meanings of these transactions. In this regard, it is well to recognize that
case reports are highly selective illustrations rather than scientific

data—the latter require verbatim reports of entire sessions and sequences of sessions.

Finally, there needs to be a detailed description of the patient's material that emerges after the deviation has or has not been acceded to by the therapist. Unconscious reactions to touch may be immediate or may be delayed until the following one or two sessions. Care to include all of the patient's dreams and stories— and to obtain and report associations to these narratives—is especially important.

Given that touch between patient and therapist is a ground rule issue, it is striking to see the extent to which writers neglect to present the nature of the frame conditions of the psychotherapy in which this issue arose and the kinds of interventions that they have made prior to the patient's entreaty. Also noteworthy are the therapist-imposed restrictions of the interchanges that surround these incidents to manifest and intellectualized discussions in which patients' narrative communications are shut off, minimized, or not given their full due. When dreams do appear, they are discussed in terms of their manifest contents and not considered to reflect encoded unconscious perceptions of the therapist and his or her touch-related interventions. Trigger decoding is nowhere to be found. In addition, narrative associations to dreams are scarce or absent, even though the SAA has found that associations to dream elements tend to be far more powerful and telling than the dream itself. As for issues of death and death anxiety, even though such material does emerge in these clinical reports, they are not considered in depth in formulating the interactional causes of requests for this type of contract and certainly are not seen as basic to what has transpired for either the patient or the therapist.

In this regard, studies of both patients and therapists from the SAA vantage-point indicate that recent death-related traumas and unresolved death anxiety play a basic role in both a patient's request for physical contact with the therapist and in the therapist's responses to that request. This type of frame violation is always in part a frame deviant effort to deny death and often functions unconsciously as a frame-deviant way of alleviating any of the three forms of death anxiety in either the patient or therapist, or both. Thus, in the face of existential death anxiety, touch is a way of denying loss and personal mortality; for predator death anxiety, it is a guilt-motivated attempt to be harmed and punished; and for predatory death anxiety, it is a way to deny the violence that is being directed at and unconsciously experienced by one member of the therapeutic dyad by the other member.

These kinds of problems are inherent to the prior literature on this subject and are reflected in all of the papers that I have reviewed—they are intrinsic to conscious system psychotherapy and psychoanalysis. Those who argue for the need for a therapist to touch some patients some of the time tend to justify their position using consciously orientated ideas and clinical observations in which deep unconscious experience and wisdom, and trigger decoding, play no role whatsoever. Touch is rationalized as an antidote to severe early traumas, maternal deprivation, attachment needs, as a corrective against patients' fear of non-sexual physical contact, as a corrective emotional experience, as a way of teaching patients new ways to relate, as a way of accepting the patient, and the like. Patients' request for physical holding are taken at face value and the unconscious sources of these requests, especially contributions from their therapists, receive little or no attention.

## Clinical material

I conclude this chapter by presenting an illustrative vignette that is discussed from the vantage-point of the SAA and then offer some final clinical and theoretical precepts in respect to the SAA approach to touch between patients and therapists. I am, however, limited in regard to the clinical material that I can turn to in offering an illustrative vignette. One of the basic ground rules of psychotherapy calls for the total privacy and confidentiality of a psychotherapy experience, and in respect for these ground rules, SAA therapists do not present their own case material. I shall therefore offer a single case illustration drawn from a previously published psychotherapy case study in which physical contact played a role (Langs, 1985). The material is drawn from a series of in-depth, three-hour exploratory interviews with former psychotherapy patients; the purpose of these interviews was an attempt to define the curative and harmful factors that hold sway in various forms of psychotherapy and psychoanalysis.

The former patient, whom I call Mr Edwards, was a married man who was in psychotherapy with a woman social worker, Ms Elton. This was his third treatment experience, primarily for chronic depression, which had begun after the death of his mother some years earlier.

The basic framework of the once weekly therapy had many departures from the unconsciously validated ideal frame. Mr Edwards worked in the same social welfare organization as Ms Elton (a violation of the therapist's relative anonymity and of the rule that calls for confinement of contact between patient and therapist to the therapist's office and the appointed hours). She had her office in the basement of her home where, after she married, her husband let the patient in for his sessions (a further violation of the therapist's relative anonymity and of the ground rules that call for the total privacy of the psychotherapy and for the therapist's office to be in professional building and not connected with the therapist's living quarters). Ms Elton also allowed Mr Edwards to accumulate a large debt of unpaid fees that she wrote off when he wrote a final essay that she needed to complete a course that she was taking (a violation of the ideal fee arrangements that call for the patient to be current with his fee payments and a violation of the basic purpose of the therapy and of the restriction of the therapist's satisfactions in doing the therapy to her fee and intangibles related to healing the patient). After the patient had an affair with a female co-worker, this therapist took her into therapy using the time directly after Mr Edwards' weekly sessions (a violation of the total privacy of the therapy).

Additional departures from the ideal frame included self-revelations by Ms Elton regarding her personal life, her reports to Mr Edwards on the comments made by a therapist to whom she went for supervision for his case, and their exchanging gifts. Finally, prior to the incident to be described below, the therapist had made several offers to hold the patient's hand, which he had refused.

Well into the therapy, Ms Elton announced that she finally understood the patient's problem but was reluctant to tell him what it is as yet. After cajoling her to do so, she finally said to Mr Edwards, "You, my dear man, are a child."

Mr Edwards began to cry uncontrollably and this time he accepted Ms Elton's offer to hold his hand and stroke his arm. She then told the patient that when she broke up with one of her boyfriends, she had been as deeply hurt as the patient was now, and she described what had happened. Mr Edwards began to settle down and proceeded to go over the many ways that he is indeed childlike. At the end of the hour, he thanked his therapist for her support and for being there for him, and he left the session feeling reassured that he'd just experienced a major breakthrough in his therapy.

That night he had a dream in which he is in a cavern. Two white hands come up through the floor, grab hold of his hand and try to pull him down and under in order to destroy him. Terrified, he fights off the hands.

In connection with later sessions in which the therapist again held the patient's hand or kissed him goodbye, the patient had associations to his own promiscuity, to his illicit affairs, and when the therapist moved her office to a new neighbourhood, to the area being frequented by prostitutes. In talking about the physical contact in his interview with me, he moved from alluding to the physical contact with Ms Elton— which consciously he had found helpful, caring, and comforting—to images of himself as needing sex with a lot of women because of his own sexual insecurities and as a way of undoing his feelings of depression, as having taken to dressing his wife in the same clothing that his therapist wore, as making many mistakes in his work, and as a poorly informed therapist who should be doing some other kind of work.

This material demonstrates the striking differences between patients' conscious and unconscious perceptions of physical contacts with their therapists. Manifestly and consciously, most patients accept this contact with appreciation and as a sign of their therapists' concerns for them. But in their encoded communications, their view of the therapist is quite the opposite—therapists are seen as exploiting the patient, prostituting themselves, trying to harm or murder the patient, and attempting to undo their own pathology and relieve themselves of emotional symptoms at the expense of the patient. What is seen as a correct intervention consciously is seen as a dire error unconsciously, and a positive conscious view of the therapist's efforts is accompanied by a negative one unconsciously. All in all, a seemingly helpful intervention on the conscious level is experienced as devastatingly destructive deep unconsciously.

Discovering these universal truths lies in the listening—in taking touch-related interventions as the triggers for patients' subsequent narrative material and decoding its themes as unconscious perceptions of the actual implications of the intervention.

No single case can stand as representative of all cases or as any kind of proof of a clinical position. The material I have offered here has limitations in that it is based on a recorded interview. While I did not touch this interviewee except to greet him and thank him at the end of the interview, it is quite certain that all of the terrible encoded images that he generated in associating to Ms Elton's physical contacts with him encoded the harmful aspects of my well intended but nevertheless frame violating recorded interview with him. In addition, it can be argued that the negative thematic material is so severe because of the other frame violation in which the therapist engaged or that it pertains more to those frame deviations than it does to the physical contact. My position also may be challenged with the possibility that destructive unconscious perceptions of their therapists' interventions need not be harmful to patients, who may do well clinically despite these unconscious experiences. And finally, the question could be raised in light of my earlier comments as to why issues of death anxiety are not prominent in this vignette.

My only response to these challenges, which I believe to be largely unfounded, is to suggest that the absence of death-related material in this interview is most probably a function of my own unconscious defensiveness and an example of how theory directs data gathering—and may, of course, either prejudice the data collection or facilitate gathering the critical information needed to understand a given therapeutic interlude. In the self-processing psychotherapy that I do (Langs, 1993, 2004a,b), there seldom is a session without powerful frame issues—they arise in both modified and secured psychotherapies. On this basis, death-related anxieties of one kind or another are activated, death-related material presses for expression, and unconscious defences directed against their expression are mobilized in response. In most sessions, patients do communicate material that allows for interpretation and frame rectification when called for.


## Deep unconscious understandings of physical contact

I conclude by summing up my experiences and insights as a supervisor of psychotherapy in regard to the occasional sessions that I have supervised in which physical contact between a patient and therapist took place. Universal patterns and trends have emerged in regard to patients' experiences and therapists' needs that pertain to these events—a central set of core findings with individual variations in particular patients and therapists.

Therapists' touching their patients may be consciously motivated by helpful reasons and accepted as such by patients. Nevertheless, physical contact in psychotherapy is a frame modification that is deeply unconsciously perceived by both parties to the contact as seductive, incestuous, harmful or murderous, punishing and imprisoning, predatory and inappropriate, and in error.

Touch between patients and therapists tends to have unconsciously mediated harmful effects on both parties. These effects tend to be missed because consciously both individuals usually deny the consequent symptomatic regressions, fail to link them to the physical contact, miss the indications and narrative that allude to the unconscious processing that transpires. In addition, therapists in particular fail to make use of the trigger decoding efforts that would reveal their patients' deep unconscious responses to the touch interlude.

Deeply unconsciously, patients tend to accept or request physical contact with their therapists because their therapists have structured their therapies in a frame-deviant manner. The invocation of frame violations becomes the prevailing mode of coping with death anxieties and deep unconscious conflicts—however costly they may be. Patients also accept physical contact because of deep unconscious guilt over having harmed others in the past and they ask to be touched as an unconsciously mediated form of punishment. Patients with histories of severe early traumas and those who experience the world in primitive and terrifying ways also accept touch as a way of avoiding the narrative expression of their traumas and their usually violent and sexually assaultive unconscious views of themselves and others. In this way, acting in through physical contact with their therapists serves to preclude the communication of their dreaded narratives, however encoded they may be.

Deeply unconsciously, therapists tend to accept or initiate physical contact with their patients as a way of alleviating their own death anxieties. This may pertain to early death-related traumas or to a recent death-related illness or injury, significant loss, or other kind of death-related event. Touch also is used by therapists after failures at intervening or following harmful interventions, serving as a way of precluding the expression of patients' extremely critical responsive encoded narratives. Touch also is a form of action-discharge that expresses therapists' deep unconscious needs to seduce or harm their patients in ways that they can consciously rationalize and deny. Touch also may be invoked in the service of therapists' deep unconscious guilt for having harmed their patients and others. In these instances, the harmful prior behaviour or intervention usually is perceived unconsciously rather than consciously and touch is invoked as a way of inviting punitive responses from the patient, such as provoking him or her to leave treatment.

## Matters of technique regarding physical contact

Patient–therapist touch may arise either deliberately at the request of one or the other party, or may occur inadvertently. With inadvertent physical contact, the therapist should keep the incident in mind as a trigger. That is, he or she must bear primary responsibility for these accidental moments of touch and the patient role is secondary. (Patients' frame breaks are termed patient-indicators, and they too are processed by his or her deep unconscious system and interpreted accordingly; Langs, 2004a.)

In the session following the physical contact, the therapist should continue to keep it in mind as the trigger, and trigger-decode the patients' narrative material in light of that event—treating the themes as reflections of valid unconscious perceptions of the implications of what had happened. Patients often fail to consciously experience this kind of contact and, even when they do, they seldom mention it in their sessions. If necessary, then, after obtaining meaningful encoded material, the therapist should allude to the trigger—i.e., to the accidental physical contact—in interpreting the patients' deep unconscious experience of the incident.

Therapists who have thoughts of inviting touch between themselves and their patients should refrain from mentioning the urge to, or carrying it out with, the patient. Such wishes are the private concern and problem of the therapist and call for extensive self-processing (Langs, 1993, 2004a). As noted, death-related issues in the therapist's life, and often in the patient's material, are almost certain to be at the root of this inappropriate, frame-violating desire in the therapist.

When patients suggest that they be held or touched by their therapists, the therapist's response should be attentive silence or the request that the patient continue to say whatever is coming to mind. It is inappropriate to unilaterally comply or refuse—i.e., for the therapist to state his or her intentions in either direction—or to share with the patient any uncertainties about what he or she should or will do. This sharing is self-revealing and a violation of the therapist's anonymity and neutrality and often, it is unconsciously experienced by the patient as making touch a likely outcome.

Instead, sound, unconsciously validated technique calls for the therapist to intervene on the basis of the patient's encoded deep unconscious directives. Thus, the therapist should wait for—and foster if need be—their patients' emerging encoded narratives, such as dreams or stories. This material, understood in light of the patient's request for this frame modification, will point to the trigger from the therapist that has evoked the request—it always is an interactional event with contributions from both therapist and patient (Langs, 2004a). It also will reveal the deep unconscious meanings for the patient of the therapist's response, be it compliance or non-compliance—and always will speak for and encode the need to keep the frame secured and not touch the patient.

It is well to appreciate, then, that the deep unconscious wisdom subsystem of the emotion-processing mind has the capability of managing the ground rules of psychotherapy with utter brilliance and entirely in the service of emotional healing. When the issue of touch arises, the patient's deep unconscious wisdom subsystem will not only accurately perceive the ramifications of the therapist's acquiescing or not, it also will adaptively process the issue and encode a clear directive against physical contact. This is an example of the not uncommon situation in which the deep unconscious wisdom subsystem knows best, and this holds true for patients' narrative material in their sessions, as well as therapists' own, privately considered encoded narratives.

## Conclusion

I want to emphasize that the emotional universe that is mapped and explored by conscious system forms of psychotherapy and psychoanalysis is a world in which manifest contents and their implications are the main sources of understanding and intervening. The SAA is a deep unconscious mode of treatment in which manifest contents are given their full due, but encoded narratives are the main source of information and meaning. This provides access to a distinctive emotional universe in which consistencies, archetypes, universals, frame issues, and empowered meanings hold sway. It is for this reason that other therapists strongly disagree about the effects of physical contact between patients and therapist, while SAA therapists are unequivocal in their conviction that such events cause far more deep and lasting, unconsciously mediated harm than healing. Personally, in all my years as an SAA therapist and supervisor, I have never come across a deep unconscious mind that favours this frame violation and have trigger-decoded countless encoded narratives that speak to the seductiveness and damage wrought by this frame violation.

# CHAPTER ELEVEN

# A body psychotherapist's approach to touch

*Nick Totton*

> "In a relationship where passing a box of Kleenex can be ill-advised at certain times, touching the patient's body undoubtedly can create a complex web of repercussions. This is no reason to eschew touching. It means, however, that the therapist's goals and reasons must be absolutely clear and uncomplicated by his or her own personal needs"
>
> (McNeely, 1987, p. 78)

I am writing from a very different position to that of other contributors to this volume, in that I am a practising body psychotherapist. I trained as a Reichian therapist, in the direct tradition of Wilhelm Reich. My original training (with Energy Stream, the Post Reichian Therapy Association) was "humanistic Reichian", following the near-universal picture of Reich as a "growth movement" practitioner that developed in the 1950s and subsequently.

However, although Reich was excluded from the psychoanalytic movement in the 1930s (for an account see R. Jacoby, 1986), his work was developed within psychoanalysis—in fact, in an effort to cleave to what Reich saw as the fundamental orientation of psycho-analysis towards the body and its energy. When I did an MA in Psychoanalytic Studies in the 1990s, I came to realize how completely Reich's work was rooted in Freudian ideas, and how much more sense it made in that context (Totton, 1998). I now understand my own practice as, in effect, "analytic body psychotherapy". In fact, I call the style of work that I teach and practise, "Embodied–Relational Therapy"; in what follows I will be referring sometimes to body psychotherapy in general, and sometimes to Embodied–Relational Therapy in particular. I shall do my best to keep the distinction clear.

Contrary to widespread belief, body psychotherapy (Totton, 2003) is not synonymous with touch; it can be, and often is, carried out with no physical contact between client and therapist. Sometimes therapists share with clients what they perceive about the client's body posture, movements, expressions, and so on, together with their own associations. Sometimes they suggest ways in which clients might develop or otherwise explore what is happening in their body. Sometimes they mirror clients' movements or posture, and this can develop into an active exchange. Sometimes, if they take a more adjustment-orientated approach, they offer clients exercises and postures intended to increase their range of movement, free their breathing, or facilitate the flow of energy. And sometimes they simply hold their own embodied experience as a resource of information about the client's process. None of these activities implies touch; many of them are used occasionally by practitioners who do not identify themselves as body psychotherapists.

However, probably only a fairly small number of body psycho-therapists systematically refrain from touching their clients in the way that probably a large majority of verbal psychotherapists do. Rothschild (2000) is one of that small number. Body-orientated practitioners tend to feel comfortable with their own embodiment, and comfortable with physical contact—trusting their ability to hold appropriate boundaries without avoiding touch altogether. And beyond this generally touch-positive attitude, many (but not all) body psychotherapists regularly use specific techniques in their work that are based on physically touching clients.

In this chapter, I distinguish five different ways in which touch can be used in psychotherapy, all of which I see as in principle legitimate, and discuss their clinical function, together with potential clinical pitfalls. Some of these uses of touch are specific to body psychotherapy, and probably require specialized training, others are not, and do not. After looking at these five kinds of touch, I discuss touch in therapy from an ethical point of view.

## Five levels of touch

### 1. Touch as comfort

The most basic use of touch in psychotherapy—whether body-orientated or otherwise—is as a way of offering comforting and supportive contact. Many people in our society are starved of such contact; it has a profound healing function all on its own. Touch deprivation is, in our culture, an almost universal form of early trauma. It has been well demonstrated that,

> Laboratory animals who are given rich tactile experiences in their infancy grow faster, have heavier brains, more highly developed myelin sheaths, bigger nerve cells, more advanced skeletal muscular growth, better coordination, better immunological resistance, more developed pituitary/adrenal activity, earlier puberties, and more active sex lives than their isolated genetic counterparts. [Juhane, 1987, p. 49]

There is no reason to doubt that the same is true for humans; and also that more complex emotional and social damage is caused by touch deprivation (Montagu, 1971)—which, as well as being endemic in many Western families, is also encouraged or even enforced by many medical regimes around childbirth (Prescott, 1971). Prescott, a neuropsychologist, collated information on 400 tribal societies to show that, "those societies which give their infants the greatest amount of physical affection were characterized by low theft, low infant physical pain, low religious activity, and negligible or absent killing, mutilating, or torturing of the enemy" (Prescott, 1975, p. 12) and that, "deprivation of body pleasure throughout life—but particularly during the formative periods of infancy, childhood, and adolescence—[is] very closely related to the amount of warfare and interpersonal violence" (*ibid.*, p. 14).

Hugging a client in distress, or holding their hand or their head, can be seen as a basic human response, and is treated in that way by many humanistic therapies; one suspects that it also happens far more often than is talked about even in the psychoanalytic tradition, where it has been frowned on ever since Freud censured Ferenczi in 1931 for—supposedly—kissing patients (Freud & Ferenczi, 2000; Grosskurth, 1991).

Freud's major concern at the time seems to have been about bad publicity; but later analytic objections have centred around the concept of "gratification", drawing on passages in Freud's writings like the following:

> ... I shall state it as a fundamental principle that the patient's need and longing should be allowed to persist in her, in order that they may serve as forces impelling her to do work and make changes, and that we must beware of appeasing those forces by means of surrogates. [Freud, 1915a, p. 165]

It is suggested, therefore, that touch offers a gratification of the client's desires which is therapeutically counter-productive: that it offers the client—and sometimes the empathic practitioner—an escape from painful feelings which it would be better to stay with and experience.

Realistically, however, psychotherapy must always work in a state of tension between some degree of "gratification"—for example, greeting the client at the start of the session—and some degree of "deprivation"—for example, ending the session on time. On to this mixed reality the client will project a scenario of giving or withholding, hate or love, which corresponds to their history and expectations; this, after all, is what we call "transference". As Ferenczi said of his "twofold method of frustration and indulgence": "However great the relaxation, the analysis will not gratify the patient's actively aggressive and sexual wishes or many of their other exaggerated demands. There will be abundant opportunity to learn renunciation and adaptation" (Ferenczi, 1930, p. 441).

The issue of touch as comfort, then, becomes essentially one among many technical issues, with important and subtle questions to be asked in each specific case about usefulness, appropriateness, timing, and so on (c.f. Hunter & Struve, 1997; Tune, 2005). The central issue, as Mario Jacoby emphasizes, ". . . is the analyst's capacity to imagine in an empathic way beforehand what physical touching might mean to the patient" (M. Jacoby, 1986, p. 123). He does sometimes offer bodily contact to his clients, when the client is so locked away that

> Whatever the analyst would say would be wrong. And just sitting silently may be felt as if he or she is not there. It can be an experience of torture for the analysand. Thus the impulse to reach the patient by some direct physical touch seems appropriate. [M. Jacoby, 1986, p. 122]

D. W. Winnicott, though silent about touch in his writings, is well known to have used it as an aid to and a support through regression. "Literally, through many long hours he held my two hands clasped between his, almost like an umbilical cord . . ." (Little, 1985, p. 21; see the section below on regression). Other analysts, while certainly just as moved by their clients' pain, argue that touch is never the best way forward. For example, Patrick Casement (1982, 1985) describes a situation where a client in deep distress put tremendous psychological pressure on him to hold her hand. He refused, for reasons that included his perception that the original trauma which the client was exploring involved the *absence* of her mother's touch; for the therapist to offer his hand would therefore tend to suppress, rather than facilitate, a therapeutic reliving of the trauma. It would also, Casement felt, have given the message that he could not bear her suffering, and needed to stop it. In the end, both client and therapist agreed that the real need was not to *be* touched, but to experience him as "*in* touch" with her suffering.

Any therapist who offers physical comfort should read Casement's argument against it—especially if they come from the humanistic context, where the complexity of the situation and the need for restraint are perhaps not always taken seriously enough. I disagree, though, with Casement's view that physical holding will *always* be less creative than purely verbal and empathic "holding". Some people, at some times, are so structured that they cannot *feel* symbolic holding; only literal holding will get through. Casement himself acknowledges that it is unhelpful "to look for security in a rigid adherence to the usual rules of technique" (Casement, 1985,

p. 155), and that it is occasionally necessary to "introduce an exception" (*ibid.*); other analysts, however, insist that more than fleeting
physical contact is incompatible with psychoanalysis (e.g., Limentani, 1989, p. 244)—and indeed Wilhelm Reich himself, the founder
of body psychotherapy, was orthodox enough to see comforting
touch as "seductive" and not to be encouraged (Sharaf, 1983).

I have offered many clients occasional hugs or handholding to
comfort them at times of extreme distress. There have also been
many clients whom, although my impression of their pain has been
just as powerful, it has not felt right to touch—even if I may sometimes have an intense desire to do so. It is as if there is a "force
field" around them telling me to keep out, telling me that they are
not, at that moment, able to receive comforting touch on its own
terms, either because they need to hold on to their sense of
defended separateness, or because their history will lead them to
interpret touch as sexual and abusive.

When it has been possible later to discuss these feelings, the
client has usually confirmed my intuition—except when, very occasionally, it has transpired that they did indeed have the "Don't
touch me" reaction I experienced, but were also aware of hoping
that I would push through the force field and touch them anyway.
Their feedback has been very helpful in several ways—including
the confirmation that I am not simply touching for my own gratification or to relieve my own distress. It also raises an important
general point about touch: if it happens, it needs to be *explicitly
discussed*, afterwards if not before. Any implication that this is
something about which one should keep quiet, or something to be
kept secret from others, will inevitably raise the spectre of abuse. (In
fact, I would recommend any client whose therapist takes such an
attitude to seriously question what is going on.)

There have been a few clients over the years with whom
comforting touch has become a central part of our work together. I
want to describe one of these clients—though, like other case
vignettes which follow, this is a fictionalized and generic account
(see Denman, 2004, for a clear and concise discussion of this solution to the difficulties of writing about clients). "Angela" and I had
worked together for about three years before we had any physical
contact: she was a good example of the sort of client I referred to
earlier, who carries an excluding force field with them. Over this

period of once-a-week therapy, what gradually emerged was an extreme psychological fragility that had been concealed under a fairly robust outer persona. Angela could be described, in fact, as a "borderline personality"; and as she very gradually came to trust me, she showed more and more of her fearful and rageful underlying experience.

As this happened, I started to sense more and more of an impulse in myself to hold her, and also a change in her own attitude (earlier in the work she had several times hidden from me behind a chair, or asked me to close my eyes because my gaze was too disturbing). This crystallized decisively one day when she talked about a young boy who had turned up on her doorstep, and fantasized that he was "looking for someone to adopt him". I said, "I wonder whether you are looking to be adopted—maybe you want me to adopt you." She said, "Yes, maybe. I'd like to be your daughter. What would it mean? Would I be able to be cuddled by you?"

We spent ten or twelve sessions after this not touching, but exploring all the elements of this fantasy, and talking about what I could and could not offer, and what it would mean to us both. It would take much too long to describe the whole of this process, but eventually Angela was coming for two one-and-a-half-hour sessions a week, and spending long parts of each session being held by me as we talked. The parameters were that on each occasion she had to explicitly ask me to come and sit on the sofa with her, and ask for any touch she wanted—for example holding her hand or putting my arm around her.

Looking back, I see two main functions for this way of proceeding. First, it helped Angela be able to stay in therapy, while this deepened to the point where she could hardly endure the spaces between sessions, or the end point of each session, so powerfully restimulated was her experience of loneliness and deprivation. Touch offered her a literal and symbolic "holding" which made it just possible for her to leave each time, and to come back despite her anger at the suffering she experienced in between. Second, it allowed her to explore her need for holding and her capacity to choose and control how and when it would happen. She had many early experiences of being overwhelmed and invaded by physical contact; and the somewhat artificial parameters that I have described made it possible for her to create a separation between comfort and invasion which had not previously been available to her.

## 2. Touch to explore contact

This second theme leads me on to a further function of touch in body psychotherapy beyond that of comfort: the deliberate exploration of the client's response either to physical contact, or to the *idea* of physical contact. In other words, the therapist might ask the client whether she can put a hand on his chest, for example, and then encourage him to stay with the feelings and sensations that this contact evokes—anything from safety and relaxation to invasion and anxiety. If it seems likely that the response will be closer to this latter end of the spectrum, the therapist may, instead of actually touching the client, invite him to *imagine what it would be like* to be touched.

Both these sorts of exploration will, of course, only happen in a context that gives them relevance, for example when the client is talking about his attitudes towards physical contact. They may be a prelude to and preparation for further kinds of work with touch, like those outlined below; or they may equally well be an end in themselves, a means of opening up important life issues.

A client comes to mind whom I will call "Elizabeth" (again this account is composite and fictionalized). Elizabeth had severe eczema, and worked as a counsellor for people with skin conditions; unlike a number of my clients, she came to me specifically because she knew that I was a body psychotherapist. However, at the first and subsequent sessions, she would arrive in the room, throw herself down full length on the sofa, and begin to free associate! Despite coming for "body psychotherapy"—and I did not yet really know what that might signify to her—what Elizabeth seemed to be wanting was something more like orthodox psychoanalysis.

I went through three or four sessions wrestling with some complicated reactions: the work we were doing seemed fairly useful in its own terms, but I had after all been recruited as a body psychotherapist—did I have a responsibility to keep this agenda on the table somehow? It was not easy to get even a word in edgeways, let alone anything else. Eventually, though, Elizabeth began talking about a bodily symptom, a tension in her throat and neck. I suggested that I move my chair closer so that I could see better what was happening in her throat.

This produced a reaction of panic and freezing. Little was said for the rest of the session; but Elizabeth came back next time, and we explored the meanings of her response. For the rest of the time we worked together, I never actually did move any closer, let alone touch her; but the *theme* of closeness and touch, including its relation with her eczema, was central to our work. It became clear that Elizabeth had indeed come for "body psychotherapy", but of this very specific kind. If we had met together for years rather than for months, some sort of physical contact might or might not have occurred, who can say; but the *possibility* of touch, rather than its actuality, was a vital component of the therapy. She needed, that is, to come to a therapist who she knew *might* touch her.

## 3. Touch as amplification

Touch can be used as a basic method to focus and bring attention to bodily sensations. If the client reports a response in some particular part of the body, then the therapist—so long as it has already been established that touch is acceptable in the work with this client—may ask whether she can put a hand there. This contact generally serves to keep the client's awareness with their bodily experience, and to act as a support for exploring sensation.

At the same time, through her hands the therapist will be forming her own impression of what is happening at this site in the client's body, using what Johnson (2000) calls "intricate tactile sensitivity" to assess the degree of tension or relaxation, the quality of tissue density and tone, pulsations and micro-movements, etc.; the opportunity opens up for feedback between the client's self-perception and the therapist's observation through touch.

Here is a very simple example of touch as amplification from a recent session. The client came in with a sense of pressure and breathlessness in his chest. With his agreement, I put my open hand on his sternum and leant into him until he felt that the external pressure matched what he had been feeling internally; he growled in protest, the growl became a roar, and he connected with anger about various "pressures" he was currently feeling in his life. At the same time, through my touch I experienced a stuck, stuffy, bulky quality in his chest that, as he expressed anger, transformed into a much more vibrant and vital feeling; we were able to develop a new shared emotional vocabulary from a discussion of these perceptions.

## 4. Touch as provocation

In some forms of body psychotherapy—notably several in the Reichian tradition—intensive forms of physical pressure are used on rigid muscles, pressing, poking, "strumming", tickling, and otherwise seeking to provoke discharge. The understanding here is that we tense up our muscles in childhood as an integral part of repressing intolerable or unacceptable emotions. Once this becomes an habitual and chronic pattern, it is the muscular spasticity which in effect keeps the feeling unconscious, and which must be released in order to re-own the buried feeling (Reich, 1942).

> To mobilize a chronically contracted muscle one must first increase the contraction to a point which cannot be maintained. The muscle thus overstrained must relax. . . . Direct pressure is the usual and most effective means. One will find near the insertion of the muscle a very sensitive spot where contraction is greatest and it is here that the muscle responds best to stimulus. . . . Groups of muscles that form a functional unit in holding back emotions are worked on together. . . [Baker, 1980, p. 47]

In combination with this sort of pressure, the client might be encouraged to make expressive movements—including hitting out, kicking, squeezing, biting, ripping, clawing, pulling, pushing—generally using a cushion; and to moan, shout, growl, scream, and so on: "If it hurts, make a noise about it". The sound may start off mechanically or in reaction to physical pain, but if the work is done skilfully then the deeper emotional connection is made with the repressed feelings being "held" in the tight muscles. This is what differentiates such work from intensive massage: emotional and conceptual links are being made between what Reich called "muscular armouring", and psychological blocks and inhibitions. Very frequently powerful images will spontaneously emerge which resonate on many levels through the subsequent therapy (Totton, 1998).

## 5. Touch as skilled intervention

Many body psychotherapists have a range of bodywork skills which they sometimes employ with their clients. These might include techniques from osteopathy, acupressure, shiatsu, craniosacral therapy, various forms of massage, and many other disciplines. Some of these are taught as part of certain body psychotherapy trainings; others, the individual practitioner will have learnt independently and synthesized with their own body psychotherapy practice.

This is an area of some potential difficulty for body psychotherapy: it raises tricky questions about its relationship with the sorts of body therapies that place themselves within complementary medicine. What will be the effect on the transference–countertransference relationship of the therapist employing specifically "curative" skills with the client? The best parallel I can find within psychotherapy in general is the medically-qualified therapist or analyst who prescribes antidepressants for a client: it would be widely agreed that this sort of intervention has a drastic impact upon the therapeutic relationship, fixing the practitioner firmly in the role of expert healer.

In both cases, however, it is plausible that the effect can be brought into awareness and worked with in potentially useful ways. This may in fact possibly be easier with bodywork approaches using a "complementary" paradigm, which may be more empowering for the client than the orthodox medical paradigm.

Body psychotherapy itself also has its own unique forms of skilled intervention through touch. The work on pressure points that I described above is one example, and there are many more, each specific to one or more schools. It may be useful if I briefly describe some the ways I myself work, which have developed out of the Reichian tradition in which I originally trained.

## Breath and touch

Bodywork in Embodied–Relational Therapy centres on breathing and relationship, posing the odd-sounding but fundamental question: how can I breathe and relate to someone at the same time? Whenever we have difficult feelings in relation to someone, we restrict our breathing to suppress those feelings (often quite unconsciously). Alternatively, to keep breathing, we cut off relating, for example by turning away or closing our eyes. Trying to stay open both internally and externally leads us to core therapeutic issues, immediately foregrounding transference—and also countertransference: this intense face-to-face relating combined with attention to the breath is highly demanding for the therapist as well as for the client.

When one tries to allow the breath to happen freely while attending to it consciously, consciousness and spontaneity begin to interfere with each other: resistance emerges, corresponding to repression and embodied in the breath. Breathing is right on the interface between voluntary and autonomic function: any attempt to "control ourselves"—which is largely what repression is—emerges in the breath. This seems to be at least part of why many schools of meditation are centred on attention to the breath: it is through breath control that we create and maintain what I have called "the spastic I"—the ego that is based in body *tension* rather than in body *awareness*.

The central focus of embodied–relational bodywork, then, is on re-establishing a fuller, more spontaneous breath—not by exerting effort, but by gradually letting go of our need to protect ourselves from feeling by not breathing. Working systematically through all the levels of resistance to spontaneous breath—to "being breathed"—therapist and client encounter all the familiar relationship issues that emerge through free association, or indeed any other sustained encouragement to let things happen spontaneously and without censorship.

Touch will very frequently feature in this sort of work—as contact, as comfort, as emotional expression—but also I am using touch to free the energy flow in the body, to allow the breath to move more deeply through the organism. Through training and experience, I have developed "intricate tactile sensitivity" to a range of subtle sensations from the client's body, and also the ability to turn these sensations into rich imagery, which in turn informs my touch. So, when a client has allowed their breath to take them into deep realms of non-verbal bodily expression, I will be accompanying them, largely through my touch, and using it to amplify and support their bodily impulses and flow of energy.

I am really not sure how any of this will sound to someone who has not experienced it themselves. Perhaps it comes across as mystical nonsense (Reich believed that mysticism is misunderstood bodily experience). The same is often true of mainstream psychoanalytic accounts of the extraordinary realms of shared reality into which analysts and patients can venture together: unless we have been there, it all sounds very peculiar! As a potential bridge, I recommend the respected analyst Michael Eigen's (1993) brief account of his own experience of body psychotherapy as a client; this work, he says, "supplemented my personal analysis and opened ways of experiencing I otherwise might not have reached" (Eigen, 1993, p. xviii).

## Regression

As I have already indicated, the issue of touch is closely bound up with that of regression. In the words of John Conger: "Touch is our earliest language, and capable of taking us back instantaneously to our most primitive universe" (Conger, 1994, p. 13). In this and other ways—in its whole strategy of turning the client's attention to his or her body—it seems reasonable to say that body psychotherapy has an inherent tendency to be regressive.

Regression has long been recognized as a powerful and valuable therapeutic tool, though a double-edged one. Although Freud was deeply suspicious of the ways in which clients could regress as an escape from therapy, his colleague Ferenczi saw it as an essential aspect of healing for severely traumatized individuals; and this positive understanding was taken up by Winnicott, who believed that for clients with a limited sense of self, regression could create the opportunity for "an unfreezing of an environmental failure situation" (Winnicott, 1955, p. 22). Winnicott's focus was on disturbances of early infant–carer relations, while Ferenczi's was on situations of gross abuse; but both saw touch as an important aspect of regressive work.

The other side of the coin of regression is *retraumatization*, where the attempt at therapeutic re-experiencing and discharge of traumatic experience succeeds only in recreating the original trauma, and in fact adding a further layer of trauma. Avoiding this is partly a matter of using appropriate pacing and supportive techniques (Levine, 1997; Rothschild, 2000); but the issue goes deeper. Ferenczi encountered this problem repeatedly in his explorations of regressive work, and concluded that it was the product of an unsafe therapeutic relationship:

> An abreaction of quantities of the trauma is not enough: the situation must be different from the actually traumatic one in order to make possible a different, favourable outcome. The most essential aspect of the altered repetition is the relinquishing of one's own rigid authority and the hostility hidden in it. [Ferenczi, 1988, p. 108]

It has been repeatedly pointed out how an atmosphere of trance-like compulsion can develop around the enactment of traumatic material in therapy. This is no less true, and perhaps even more potentially damaging, around the use of touch, just because of its regressive power. When "James" came to me (again a fictionalized and composite character), I was struck by the tension in his jaw: it fascinated me, and I felt convinced that releasing this tension would be a tremendously helpful thing that I could offer him. With his permission, I pressed strongly on the insertion point of the muscles at the hinge of his jaw, while encouraging him to breathe and make a sound. He found this unbearable, however, and very quickly asked me to stop; there was a negative effect on our relationship that lasted for more than one session.

Despite this, however, and in a state of temporary amnesia, I found myself trying exactly the same thing again a few months later—and then yet again!—each time producing a similar reaction of anger and mistrust; very understandably so. Once I managed to mobilize my awareness around this, to apologize fully and to think together with James about what was going on, we focused on his childhood experience of being repeatedly teased and physically bullied by his older brothers, and his inability to speak out about this either to them or to his parents. Both the pain of being abused, and the holding back from speaking, were held in his locked jaw.

## Ethical dimensions of touch

The strongest argument against touch in psychotherapy, it seems to me, is that in our culture touch has unavoidable overtones of sexuality and/or power. Most people's primary experiences of touch are as a child, or in a sexual context, or as a relatively disempowered petitioner for help, for example with a doctor or dentist. As John Conger points out, "In our culture, people of higher status initiate touch and touch more than those of lower status. Men touch women more than women touch men" (Conger, 1994, p. 13).

Although there are other experiences of touch possible, the entire area is enormously complex and highly charged; and it may be questioned whether a practitioner, herself a member of the same culture, can have enough clarity around touch to use it helpfully and appropriately. Touch, it is argued, will tend to sexualize the therapeutic relationship for both participants, whatever their conscious intention; and may also disempower the client in other important ways.

These are important and relevant arguments; and body psychotherapists who touch have not always taken them seriously enough. Some simply claim a pseudo-medical exemption from erotic response; ignoring the fact that medics achieve this immunity (if they do) through objectifying and alienating the bodies of their patients, treating them as meat machines. The whole direction of energy in body psychotherapy is towards a deeper and fuller appreciation of human embodiment; even if it were possible, to surgically eradicate the erotic impulse of either therapist or client would wreck the entire enterprise. In reality, such practitioners are more likely to be in denial; which is a dangerous place to be when you are touching clients.

If we are arguing for touch in body psychotherapy, we surely must acknowledge that touch between humans does indeed very strongly tend to be both erotic and regressive—that it facilitates access to the infant experience of suckling and being held and related to in a bodily way; and that this is in fact a large part of the reason for using it therapeutically. What happens and does not happen in these very early embodied relationships has a profound effect on our adult functioning (apart from numerous analytic sources, see the neuroscientific work of, for example, Schore, 2001; Trevarthen & Aitken, 2001). Working with touch enables us to reach back into this infant world in very powerfully effective ways. At the same time, though, the passage through the Oedipal field takes up and transforms infant eroticism into adult sexuality; we can never

wholly or permanently have one without the other. In acknowledging all this, we are acknowledging our own implication as practitioners in these erotic and regressive fields of force; and
acknowledging that this makes enormous demands on our
integrity, demands which at times will need every scrap of strength
we possess.

In the work which "Angela" and I did together (see above),
there came a point when her experience of my touch was no longer
wholly in the register of infancy; she began, and *needed* to begin, to
have specifically sexual feelings in response to our physical contact.
Not surprisingly, some of this was mirrored in me; the quality of my
erotic countertransference also shifted. This was frightening for
both of us. Interestingly, though, it was precisely the depth and
solidity of our touch-relationship that enabled us to weather the
crisis and actually to *explore*, on a level of sensation and fantasy,
without at any point transgressing the boundaries which the situation needed. We moved, in other words, from enacting mother–
infant dynamics to enacting father–daughter dynamics; just as
Angela had been able to nourish and heal herself on the infant level,
she was able to heal the absence in her life of a father who could
appreciate and respond to her sexuality without exploiting it
(Samuels, 1993). This work was far deeper—and, of course, far
scarier—when channelled through the medium of touch.

## Conclusion

As this story perhaps underlines, I am not advocating touch for all
therapists and all clients. It would be very unwise for a therapist to
embark on a touch relationship with a client if they are not themselves well grounded in this area, comfortable and familiar with
touch outside its familiar territory of sexuality and parenting—and
living a life that includes plenty of satisfying physical contact. More
than that, I believe that certain types of character are much more
able to tolerate the erotic stimulation of touch relationships without
needing to become actively sexual.

As for the client, bodywork, including work with touch, is
primarily useful when it can offer a bridge between "somatic" and
"psychic" modes of experience. It is most appropriate either for

clients who are already very much "in their body", and need to be met in the register of their own predominant mode of experience before exploring other registers like the verbal and intellectual; or for clients who are disconnected from their embodied selves, and who, having been met in the verbal and intellectual registers, need to explore the unknown territory of the body.

I do less hands-on bodywork now than when I started as a therapist, because I have a wider range of skills, which lets me use bodywork when, and only when, it is the best tool. Apart from fleeting social touch, I probably touch and am touched by only a minority of my clients at any point in our work together, let alone on a regular basis. The touch I do, though, is much more focused and useful. Also, it integrates much more fluidly with talking, rather than having the rather abrupt and awkward transitions that many body psychotherapists experience: "Now we will stop one sort of interaction and start another sort". I can imagine that I might some day work without touching or being touched by clients at all. But I cannot imagine working without the *possibility* of touch as an active, continuous, and creative element in my practice.

# CHAPTER TWELVE

# Something dangerous: touch in forensic practice

*Emma Ramsden, Angela Pryor, Sarita Bose,*
*Sharmila Charles, and Gwen Adshead*

"Yet have I in me something dangerous, which let thy
wisdom fear"

(*Hamlet*, Act V, Scene I)

I n this chapter, we discuss some of our experiences as therapists
in a secure forensic psychiatric hospital, working with patients
who have committed serious acts of violence. For this group,
physical touch is associated with criminal offending and physical
damage: not only in terms of the offences that brought them to the
hospital, but often in relation to their own histories of abuse and
violence as children. We discuss the importance of holding on to
touch as a powerful positive communication, and then explore the
difficulties and complexities of touch for staff working in residential forensic psychiatric settings.

The material we present comes from our work as drama therapists, nurse therapists, speech and language therapists and medical
psychotherapists. We come from different therapeutic trainings and
backgrounds but support each other in weekly group supervision.
We have used that space to reflect on the work we present here,

using psychodynamic theory to understand our patients and our responses to them.

## Rehabilitation

We know how much of our communication is via touch. This seems especially pertinent for us, working within a high-secure environment where a no-touching policy between patients and staff is the rule. Such a policy places much more emphasis on spoken language, which presents problems in a population where 75% of patients have speech, language, and communication problems (Bryan, 1998).

The hospital's role is to "care, treat and rehabilitate" patients with severe mental illness. Our patients often come to the hospital because of a fatal or destructive touching that they carried out. In their own childhood histories, touch has often been associated with cruelty, corruption, and fear. Thus, as carers and therapists, we identify with the usual embargo on touch, and most of us would start from a position that we do not use touch in our work. One of our group made the comment that, "No touch is neutral", which mirrors our experience as therapists that nothing in forensic psychotherapeutic practice is ever morally neutral.

However, what of those times and places where we do feel able to use touch in a therapeutic and rehabilitative way? One consistent finding of studies on patients with mental illness is that they have poor social skills, which persist even when their illness is pharmacologically controlled (Meuser, Bellack, Douglas, & Morrison, 1991). These patients may respond to cognitive behavioural therapy (Tarrier et al., 1998) and social skills training, both of which have been shown to be of benefit to patients with severe mental illness (Penn & Meuser, 1996). "Social skills" is an umbrella term that encompasses a number of activities, ranging from daily living to communicative behaviours. Within the forensic setting a multidisciplinary team, including occupational therapists, arts therapists, and nurses, provides rehabilitative training for both the maintenance and development of such skills.

Interpersonal skills is an area of social skills that has increasingly fallen within the remit of speech and language therapy.

Interpersonal skills are viewed as the foundation of social competence and relate to the way we express our emotions and feelings, using verbal and non-verbal communication, of which touch is just one component (Henton, Sinclair, & Sideras, 2000).

However, touch is one component that within the forensic setting leaves the speech and language therapist in a dilemma. No one would dispute that the existence of a no-touch policy exists to protect both service user and carer. However, for a professional whose role is to address touch within an interpersonal skills framework, the policy's very existence challenges our rehabilitative function. Moreover, if the policy is complied with as part of the rehabilitation process, it then serves to prevent the learning of appropriate skills, and as such, may contribute to prolonging vulnerable individuals' issues with touch, one of the most powerful components of interpersonal communication.

The acquisition of interpersonal skills is an ongoing life process, via the imitation of others, including family members, peers, and work colleagues. Formal instruction can form part of the process (for example, from teacher to pupil), but gradually individuals begin to learn how to behave and interact appropriately within their communication environment, with feedback both confirming and reinforcing behaviours.

Therefore, within the forensic mental health setting, service users appear to be in a double dilemma. First, the acquisition process of their interpersonal skills has been grossly violated, and second, the environment in which they have arrived operates within a distorted social space: an environment that does not lend itself to providing the opportunity to observe interpersonal behaviour norms.

Following an initial period of care and treatment within the hospital, an individual then embarks on a rehabilitation process, and inevitably their poor social skills lead to their participation in social skills programmes. The objectives of such programmes are to encourage such individuals to explore their communicative behaviours and move towards a more socially acceptable framework of interpersonal skills, both within a group setting and subsequently during their on/off ward activities.

The second dilemma then arises when the aspect of touch has to be addressed within the interpersonal skills rehabilitation programme. The custom of shaking hands is used as an example here. Within western culture shaking hands is both a customary form of greeting and also of marking the closure of a business meeting. However, within the forensic environment this customary and benign touch gesture would constitute a violation of the no-touching policy. Such a policy would not only prevent individuals practising such a gesture, but would prevent them from observing such behaviour within their environment, even though it constitutes a socially accepted norm within the society to which they will be released.

This then raises the question of whether a blanket no-touching policy is appropriate. Should such institutions examine their interpersonal skills more closely? So, when offered a hand by a service user, do we respond with the blanket response, "No, that is not appropriate", or should we stop and search a bit deeper? What exactly is the *function* of the offered hand? What is the function of the particular touch? How does it relate to our social norms?

If the proffered hand is a ploy by an individual to interrupt you while you are speaking to someone, and he is well aware of this, then the function of the gesture is to interrupt and is therefore inappropriate. The verbal response, "No, that is not appropriate", would then be entirely appropriate. However, if the gesture is made by a patient who is leaving the hospital the next day and wishes to say good-bye, the handshaking gesture would be functioning as a closure of business: an entirely appropriate gesture and within accepted social norms. However, we may still be unsure whether what seems appropriate in some mental health settings will be seen as entirely inappropriate within the no-touch forensic setting.

It therefore appears that the issue of touch within interpersonal exchanges is too complex in any society to be dealt with by a blanket no-touching policy, and the dilemmas it creates for those within the high secure forensic setting are real for both patients and carers alike.

### Drama therapy

Drama therapy draws upon an eclectic range of theoretical models such as the creative arts, psychology, psychotherapy, and anthropology. Underpinning its theory is a belief in the healing power of drama (Jones, 1996). The nature of using drama with groups invites with it the use of physical touch: not momentary touch, but intentional structured and spontaneous touch.

When introducing a discussion about touch in work forums, the conversation often focuses on non-consensual touch, such as violent and abusive acts between patient and patient or patient and staff. There appears to be little written on the clinical development of consensual platonic touch in psychodynamic groups, despite interest and diverse opinion among the therapeutic community. Orbach (2003a,b) has commented on the difficulty that many therapists have in exploring the momentary uses of touch that may occur between them and their patients, because touch is seen as off limits within a psychoanalytic context. She suggests that, ". . . we need to be able to . . . bring our bodies to the therapeutic encounter: to not leave them out of the relationship" (2003a, p. 13). This notion can be perceived as threatening, as it appears to demand a blurring of boundaries between professional models. Feelings of shame, confusion, and loss of control of professional and personal safety can be experienced by the therapist. These unconscious exchanges between patient and therapist are a rich area for exploration in both personal therapy and clinical supervision.

The presence of the "ideological editor" is helpful when exploring what may be present in response to patients' transference through the therapists' countertransference. The ideological editor is ". . . the way the therapist views the client through their own belief-and-value system. This includes conscious prejudice, racism, sexism and other assumptions that colour the way we miss-see, miss-hear or miss-relate to the client" (Hawkins & Shohet, 2000, p. 79).

With our colleague Mario Guarnieri we have developed a co-working model using physical touch in a dramatic psychodynamic framework in our work with offenders. In the initial stages of a group we place emphasis on playing, focusing on touching the self and then exploring touch with others. Winnicott (1971, p. 41) reminds us that ". . . playing facilitates growth and therefore health; playing leads into group relationships; playing can be a form of communication in psychotherapy . . .".

When using physical touch and play, the impact on both patients and staff needs to be sensitively worked through by the therapists prior to it starting. Many patients have experienced distorted and damaging touch experiences from primary caregivers and/or significant others early in their lives. These abusive events have shaped their inadequate interpersonal functioning, leading to a deprived understanding of empathy and the basic boundaries of consensual touch (platonic and sexual). This deprivation and absence contribute to intolerable feelings of anger and fear, which may be displaced into sexual offending and other non-consensual activities. Naitove (1988) suggests that "... sexual offenders, not unlike their victims ... have suffered a developmental arrest at some point in their maturation".

The group begins seated, with a verbal check-in. We listen to the emergent themes, assessing needs and identifying potential areas of risk and vulnerability. We then suggest working with what is present in the group. Group members are invited to stand in a circle. As this instruction is being carried out, we assess their willingness to engage, awareness of self and other and any subtle changes of physical presentation that may have occurred.

One structured touch-based exercise, which lasts between ten and fifteen minutes, focuses on interpersonal knowledge via a series of group "greetings". We have used this exercise many times, in the initial phases of groups. Members are invited to walk around the room, changing direction at will, focusing on themselves, but with an awareness of others. We ask the group to think about what it feels like to inhabit their bodies, locating any aches and pains and considering the origin of these. Reflections are not shared verbally until the exercise is complete. We develop this work by issuing a series of evenly paced instructions:

- make fleeting eye contact with others without facial expression;
- add a nod of acknowledgement;
- add a wave;
- followed by saying "good morning";
- add a one handed handshake;
- then a handshake and a wave;
- a pat on the back;
- finally an embrace.

This exercise can be a catalyst in shaping the group's direction, as individual actions have group-wide implications and can determine the group's survival or demise. Group survival may mean that use of touch through action has enabled spontaneity, leading to safe risk-taking. Positive play experiences are accessed via regressive means. As the exercise gets under way, some tomfoolery is usually present. This functions as a safety mechanism, masking embarrassment. Laughter, when its intentions are enabling and supportive, can be a helpful companion. The clarity and confident delivery of the therapist's instructions adds to group members' engagement in empathic behaviour, seeking non-verbal trust, acceptance, and respect from each and dispelling potential aggression. Tomfoolery ceases as group members focus on the therapist's narrative guidance. We stop at a pat on the back when, in our assessment at the time, the group is experiencing the exercise as too exposing.

Verbal reflections often include articulations of surprise at being able to take part in the exercise. Group members comment on their thought processes and feeling states prior to and during the exercise. We have heard comments in various groups like:

"I was really nervous and frightened";

"I enjoyed touching others";

"I thought I would crush you because you're smaller than me";

"I thought I'd panic, but I didn't";

"I haven't been held since I was a child, I miss it";

"I didn't feel so lonely whilst someone was touching me".

Creating safe and trusting boundaries takes time with this patient population due to risk factors and damaged life experiences, some of which have been discussed above. This work is long term. Group members explore their authorship of unsafe and abusive touch experiences, from the perspectives of their victims and themselves as victims by experiencing physical touch, identifying, for themselves, what is safe and unsafe. It is our hope that a group will create the possibility for transformation to be possible, towards internal change to feelings thoughts and patterns of behaviour.

## Sex offenders in a drama therapy group

Inclusion in a group that uses drama can provoke fantasies of performance anxiety, ridicule, exposure, and difficulties relating to others. These fantasies occur in the unknown space that is prior to the group's first session. To counter what can be a fragile and paralysing ego state, we offer each patient pre-group interviews and assessments in order to establish their suitability for drama therapy and to identify areas of risk and vulnerability.

Once in the group, fears can be hidden behind unconscious defences, such as withdrawal, aggression, avoidance, and flight (Barnes, Ernst, & Hyde, 1999). Often defensive warnings are made to each other, such as, "I don't want anyone to touch me, I don't like it", "I want to go back to the ward", "I'm not being touched by him". These statements are precious tools for later reflection when exploring consent.

The potential for a group of sex offenders to use the vehicle of touch to manipulate, seduce, or abuse, is real and present. As drama therapists, we share both active and witness roles throughout the group's life. As witnesses, we monitor group dynamics and risky behaviour in the group. This method of working requires a high level of support and rapport between therapists in order to work with seamless fluidity, so as to promote safety as well as psychological growth.

An understanding of the hierarchical splits present in the group, between patients whose offences were committed against adults and those who offended against children, is vital in this work. Roles inhabited include victim, perpetrator, and scapegoat. The impact of these dynamics, when working with patients who have a diagnosis of personality disorder, can potentially create splits between the therapists, as patients are unable to work through their dysfunctional ways of relating, projecting outwards on to others.

There is a possibility that the presence of touch could lead some group members to become sexually aroused, having misread and misunderstood the non-verbal signals of platonic touch between consenting adults. By safely setting up the dramatic touch work and listening to the needs of the group in terms of pace, boundaries will form which will provide enough space for the group to identify ways of containing these confusing feelings, as opposed to using them destructively. Over time, group members, will begin to gain insight, making connections between thoughts, feelings, and events both past and present.

If this arousal occurs and is known or suspected to be present by the group's therapists, it can become a thematic focus, as sexually confusing feelings are explored both verbally and by using dramatic techniques such as doubling and role play. In this event it is important to reassess the uses of touch in the group, reiterating the verbal contract for touch and seeking permission to continue using it. It may also be the case that for some group members, despite pre-group interviews, consent, and motivation to attend, they are unable to work safely with touch in the group, needing to explore these difficulties in individual therapy before returning to a group setting.

## Unwanted touching by patients and staff

Physical contact occurs frequently in the interactions between patients and nurses in a forensic psychiatric setting. However, this is rarely talked about or thought about in the day-to-day management and care of this complex group of patients.

Owing to the long average length of stay in forensic hospitals, sometimes many years, patients often form long-term relationships with nursing staff. Staff are responsible for maintaining security and therefore, in a very real sense, become attachment figures for patients. In both Bowlby's account of attachment theory and Winnicott's account of normal infant development, being held at times of fear and distress is an important function for mothers and other caregivers. As described by Hopkins (1987, 1990), the need for safe and secure touching grows as the infant becomes more distressed and frightened, "When attachment behaviour is activated at low levels it is possible for a mother to calm her infant by voice and proximity alone; but when the infant is very upset, only close physical contact can terminate distress" (1990, p. 461).

In nurse training we are taught an awareness of touch in the therapeutic relationship. Ordinarily touching someone (in a wide variety of ways) conveys to the recipient an emotional interpersonal communication. Those feeling states are wide ranging, from sympathy, love, warmth, and compassion to anger, intimidation, fear, control, and power over the other.

With good enough holding, and an experience of being psychologically contained, a child can construct an internal sense of self as competent and lovable, and a sense of others as a source of security. However, if a child experiences rejection, neglect, abuse, or abandonment, then a vital sense of internal security is lost. Most of our forensic patient population have experienced extremes of abuse, neglect, and loss as children. They may, therefore, seek out physical contact with each other or their carers either consciously or unconsciously, to make up for a sense of loss. However, if physical contact is offered, it may trigger off unconscious fear responses in the patient, causing them to reject the nurse, or even attack them, as in the following vignette.

> Mrs B was sitting on the floor in the corridor outside the smoking room. When we made eye contact, as I walked down the corridor, she smiled warmly at me and we began to talk to each other. I have known and nursed Mrs B for many years. Not thinking about my actions in this warm verbal exchange, I put my hand out to gently touch her arm as a gesture to say that it was good to see her and that I was saying goodbye for now. She responded to this by flinching and moving her body away from my reach. Contact was not made as a result of this, but she looked at me with anger and mistrust.

On reflection, the clinician was aware that she usually does not touch patients in this way because it muddles the therapeutic boundaries of the relationship. Her intention was to convey some of the warmth and good feeling she felt at seeing the patient after some months, being glad to see she was well. The patient's flinching immediately turned that warmth of feeling into a feeling that the clinician had just abused her.

This highlights the complexity and sensitivity needed to therapeutically care for people who have endured so many traumas in their earliest life. A normal, socially appropriate expression of feeling was very much unwanted by this patient. The meaning of this form of physical contact is often deeply unconscious to the patient and the member of staff. Physical contact often activates acute anxieties that the nurse—who is the primary carer and person holding the keys—is attempting to seduce them, groom them into a sexual relationship, violate the boundary of their body, and repeat earlier traumatic life events. Sometimes the patient actually touches another patient or nurse, leaving the recipient feeling that sexual overtones were expressed, but they are not consciously aware of the unconscious drive or motivation for doing so, denying that it was intended to be sexual in intention. However, the feelings the nurse may be left with are uncomfortable.

Both nurses and patients can experience each other as giving unwanted touch. Nurses may rebuff forensic patients' touch, interpreting it as possibly dangerous—in the same way as the patient above experienced touch as possibly dangerous. This can then reinforce the patients' belief that they are perpetrators, unworthy of being thought about and unlovable.

It is also the case that nursing staff do sometimes have to impose unwanted and controlling touch on a patient. A complex and emotionally stirring situation that frequently occurs in this setting can arise when a patient generates a situation of actual or imminent violence necessitating the nurses to gain a physical hold of them to prevent injury to another or themselves. At a conscious level, the nurse holding the patient by their arm or head, through learned control and restraint procedures, is very much unwanted by the patient and the nurses.

As Menzies-Lyth (1988) describes, nurses cope with their own anxieties and fears by the social defence of following procedures and policies. Consequently, using control and restraint techniques becomes a procedure and is not often thought about by the nurses or the patient involved. However, the patient, at a deeply unconscious level, is often attempting to cope psychically with acute feelings of anxiety, trauma, or loss. Often members of this patient group struggle with a more fundamental anxiety of feeling insecure and unsafe from others around them, as well as feeling unsafe from themselves and their behaviours. Patients often struggle with feelings of insecurity in that at times they feel out of control of their emotions and thoughts. One way they cope with such distress is by unconsciously using defence mechanisms such as projection or projective identification, combined with the physical act of a punch or kick, evacuating their distress. When the patient is then physically contained by the staff, he or she calms down and a sense of security is restored, in a similar way to that described above by Hopkins when the distressed infant is calmed by being held by their mother.

Often those who belong to this patient population do not have the ability to put their needs and anxieties into words and thought, just like an infant, so they ensure their survival by generating a violent incident to which the nurses must respond, ensuring that their underlying anxiety is cared for, managed, and contained. The action of physical restraint has some therapeutic value in itself, but being able to return to the patient after such a situation has occurred and talk with them about it in a non-judgemental and curious way, acknowledging their anxiety and distress, has more therapeutic value.

The role of the forensic psychiatric nurse is multi-faceted. We would argue, however, that the fundamental and primary task of any nurse working with such severe and complex psychopathologies would be the provision of a psychologically containing relationship with the patient. Physical contact in infancy is one of many vital experiences in the development of an emotionally balanced adult. When this does not happen, that adult's concept of touching others is distorted to a very severe degree. Because of unresolved traumas in infancy and childhood, patients in this setting often unconsciously re-enact abusive situations in an attempt to work through the initial trauma. If the initial trauma involves not being physically held, or is a violation of their physical body through physical or sexual abuse, those situations may be re-enacted very powerfully on the wards with other patients and with their new carers at a deeply unconscious level. Only by returning to the patient and discussing the incident with them can the patient begin to develop some meaning and ways of thinking about their psychic distress, instead of acting out their feelings on others through unwanted physical contact.

What nurses—and other mental health care professionals—perceive as unwanted physical contact often has a deeply unconscious meaning and significance for the patient and member of staff, as staff also have unconscious anxieties and fears of their own. By spending time with the patient in a calm state of mind after the event, the process of psychological containment can be completed by the caregiver to provide optimal therapeutic care and treatment.

Unwanted touch is yet another of many overt and covert communications that, if thought about in a reflective way within the patient and staff groups, can provide a deeper level of understanding of their psychopathologies, internal worlds, and defence mechanisms, ideally to provide more accurate therapeutic care and a safer working environment for everyone.

## Touching between patients in forensic residential psychiatric settings

Patients who live with each other for a very long time may use touch to express care, friendship, perhaps to feel grounded and alive in a environment that is so socially restrictive. Patients may wish to use touch to initiate relationships with other patients; this touch may be playful, friendly, or intimate.

It is when the touching goes beyond friendship that real anxieties arise. It is hardly surprising that both male and female patients should wish to have sexual relationships, some of which may be in the context of loving relationships, and some of which may be purely physical. It is also not surprising, given that 80% of our patients have experienced abuse and neglect, that they have incredible difficulty in making and maintaining intimate relationships. Successful erotic relationships rely on a robust sense of self, both psychological and physical—and few of our patients have either. Many of our male patients have come to the hospital because, for them, sex and cruelty had become fatally intertwined.

There are other reasons why psychiatric staff and institutions may resist thinking about or discussing sexual relationships between forensic patients. The forensic history indicates that sexual relationships might be dangerous for both parties; but there are more general prejudices that also operate in health care settings. There is a common assumption that mentally ill people do not have sexual desires or feelings, so that health care professionals do not take sexual histories and do not discuss the effects of illness or medication on sexual desire. In fact, it is this assumption that leads to another: namely that anyone who is ill and has sexual desire must be abnormal. Psychiatric patients therefore find two kinds of prejudice: first, it is considered abnormal for them to have desire at all, because they are ill, and second, their desires must be abnormal because they are mentally ill. If we then add to the mix the normal social prejudices against same-sex relationships, or any type of non-procreative sexual practice, it will be clear that sexual relationships between patients will be viewed with deepest suspicion.

Both staff and patients are anxious about the possibility of sexual relationships in the hospital. Nurses may want to give conscious, considered thoughts about their attitudes, beliefs, and values on the use and appropriateness of touch with patients and how they view patients' display of touch with each other. This may be influenced by the gender differences in nurses, with male nurses being sensitive to demonstrating touch through fear of how that interaction may be labelled by fellow nurses and patients. Guidelines for nurses may make carers more sensitive to distinguishing the appropriateness of touch and their willingness to use touch to as a way of showing care. It would also be helpful if staff were given an opportunity to reflect on their own sexuality and erotic sense of self, and understand how this might influence the way they relate to both male and female patients. Sadly, there is some evidence that psychiatric institutions are not supportive of this type of reflective process (Ruane, 2003).

Perhaps the issue is not about negating the use of touch with patients in a forensic setting, but about making space to think about touch, about sensitively bringing appropriate touch into the mental space between patients and their nurses/therapists. This may lead to a shared understanding of the perception of touch, and bridge the gap between the perception and the reality, thereby reducing the anxieties for carers who may want to think about the use of touch in nursing in a forensic setting.

## Conclusion

When we came to write this chapter together, we assumed that most of what we would say would be about not touching, about keeping our distance from the patients. However, despite our no-touch policy, we have found that there is a time and a place for touch in therapy, even in the forensic setting, where touch can seem dangerous.

Touching is about the crossing of a physical boundary, about the edge between two people in a space together. Even in the forensic setting, the therapeutic process is the same as anywhere else: we hope to make contact with another person and their world, and maybe bring them "on the way a little", as Bianca says in *Othello*. The forensic journey can be long for patients, staff and therapists: everyone may need a helping hand along the way.

# REFERENCES

Anderson, J. W. (1981). Interview with Margaret I. Little. 1st November. Cited in: J. W. Anderson. Winnicott the Therapist. Unpublished typescript, 1985.

Anzieu, D. (1989). *The Skin Ego*. C. Turner (Trans.). London: Yale University Press.

Baker, E. F. (1980). *Man In The Trap: The Causes of Blocked Sexual Energy*. New York: Collier.

Balint, M. (1968). *The Basic Fault: Therapeutic Aspects of Regression*. London: Tavistock.

Barnes, B., Ernst, S., & Hyde, K. (1999). *An Introduction to Groupwork: A Group-Analytic Perspective*. Basingstoke: Palgrave.

Benthien, C. (2002). *Skin: on the Cultural Border Between Self and the World*. New York: Columbia University Press.

Bick, E. (1964). Notes on infant observation in psychoanalytic training. *International Journal of Psycho-Analysis, 45*: 558–566.

Bick, E. (1968). The experience of the skin in early object-relations. *International Journal of Psycho-Analysis, 49*: 484–486.

Bowlby, J. (1988). *A Secure Base: Clinical Applications of Attachment Theory*. London: Routledge.

Briggs, A. (2002). *Surviving Space*. London: Karnac.

Bryan, K. (1998). Speech and language therapy assessment. Broadmoor Hospital January–June 1998. Lecture to Royal College of Speech and Language Therapists, Special Interest Group in Mental Health, London, November.

Carroll, R. (2003). On the border between chaos and order. In: J. Corrigall & H. Wilkinson (Eds), *Revolutionary Connections: Psychotherapy and Neuroscience*. London: Karnac.

Casement, P. (1982). Some pressures on the analyst for physical contact during the re-living of an early trauma. *International Review of Psycho-Analysis, 9*: 279–286. Also in: G. Kohon (Ed.), *The British School of Psychoanalysis: The Independent Tradition* (pp. 282–294). London: Free Association, 1986.

Casement, P. (1985). *On Learning from the Patient*. London: Routledge.

Casement, P. (2000). The issue of touch: A retrospective overview. *Psychoanalytic Inquiry, 20*: 160–184.

Conger, J. P. (1994). *The Body in Recovery: Somatic Psychotherapy and the Self*. Berkeley, CA: Frog.

Davies, J. M. (2002). Whose bad objects are we anyway? Repetition and our elusive love affair with evil. Biannual meeting of the International Association for Relational Psychoanalysis and Psychotherapy. 19 January, New York.

Decobert, S. (1984). Preface. In: A. Clancier & J. Kalmanovitch, *Winnicott and Paradox: From Birth to Creation* (pp. xi–xv). A. Sheridan (Trans.). London: Tavistock, 1987.

Denman, C. (2004). *Sexuality: A Biopsychosocial Approach*. London: Palgrave Macmillan.

Derrida, J. (1976). *Of Grammatology*. G. Spivak (Trans.). London: Johns Hopkins University Press.

Diamond, N., & Marrone, M. (2003). *Attachment and Intersubjectivity*. London: Whurr.

Dockar-Drysdale, B. (1974). My debt to Winnicott. In: *The Provision of Primary Experience: Winnicottian Work with Children and Adolescents* (pp. 1–6). London: Free Association Books, 1990.

Eigen, M. (1993). *The Electrified Tightrope*. Northvale, NJ: Jason Aronson.

Eissler, K. R. (1953). The effect of the structure of the ego on psychoanalytic technique. *Journal of the American Psychoanalytic Association, 1*: 104–143.

Farrell, E. (1989a). *Fitness Magazine*, September.

Farrell, E. (1989b). *Sunday Times*, 11 June.

Federn, P. (1953). *Ego Psychology and the Psychoses*. Oxford: Basic Books.

Ferenczi, S. (1930). The principle of relaxation and neocatharsis. *International Journal of Psycho-Analysis, 11*: 428–443 [reprinted in: J. Borossa (Ed.), *Selected Writings of Sándor Ferenczi* (pp. 275–292). London: Penguin, 1999].

Ferenczi, S. (1988). *The Clinical Diary of Sándor Ferenczi.* J. Dupont (Ed.). London: Harvard University Press.

Forer, B. R. (1969). The taboo against touching in psychotherapy. *Psychotherapy: Theory, Research and Practice, 6*: 229–231.

Frank, L. K. (1957). Tactile communication. *Genetic Psychology Monographs, 56*: 209–255.

Freud, S. (1896c). The aetiology of hysteria. *S.E., 3*: 189–221. London: Hogarth.

Freud, S. (1904a). Freud's psycho-analytic procedure. *S.E., 7*: 249–254. London: Hogarth.

Freud, S. (1912b). The dynamics of transference. *S.E., 12*: 99–108. London: Hogarth.

Freud, S. (1912e). Recommendations to physicians practising psychoanalysis. *S.E., 12*: 111–120. London: Hogarth.

Freud, S. (1913c). On beginning the treatment. *S.E., 12*: 123–144. London: Hogarth.

Freud, S. (1915a). Observations on transference-love. *S.E., 12*, pp. 159–171. London: Hogarth.

Freud, S. (1919h). The uncanny. *S.E., 17*: 219–256. London: Hogarth.

Freud, S. (1950a). Project for a scientific psychology. *S.E., 1*: 283–397. London: Hogarth.

Freud, S., & Ferenczi, S. (2000). *The Correspondence of Sigmund Freud and Sándor Ferenczi. Vol 3. 1920–1933.* E. Falzeder & E. Brabant (Eds.). Cambridge, MA: Belknap Press.

Gabbard, G. O. (1995). The early history of boundary violations in psychoanalysis. *Journal of the American Psychoanalytic Association, 43*: 1115–1136.

Gramsci, A. (1971). *Selections from the Prison Notebooks of Antonio Gramsci.* Q. Hoare & G. Smith (Trans. and Eds.). London: Lawrence and Wishart.

Greene, A. U. (2001). Conscious mind - conscious body. *Journal of Analytical Psychology 46*: 565–590.

Grosskurth, P. (1991). *The Secret Ring: Freud's Inner Circle and the Politics of Psychoanalysis.* London: Cape.

Guntrip, H. (1971). *Psychoanalytic Theory, Therapy, and the Self.* New York: Basic Books.

Hale, R., & Sinason, V. (1994). Internal and external reality: establishing parameters. In: V. Sinason (Ed.), *Treating Survivors of Satanist Abuse* (pp. 274–284). London: Routledge.

Hawkins, P., & Shohet, R. (2000). *Supervision in the Helping Professions.* Buckingham: Open University Press.

Henton, R., Sinclair, R., & Sideras, V. (2000). Interpersonal skills as part of social skill training for patients with schizophrenia. In: J. France & S. Kramer (Eds.), *Communication and Mental Illness: Theoretical and Practical Approaches.* London: Jessica Kingsley.

Hoffer, W. (1949). Mouth, hand and ego-integration. *The Psycho-analytic Study of the Child, 3–4:* 49–56.

Holder, A. (2000). To touch or not to touch: That is the question. *Psychoanalytic Inquiry, 20:* 44–64.

Holder, A. (2005). *Anna Freud, Melanie Klein, and the Psychoanalysis of Children and Adolescents.* P. Slotkin (Trans.). London: Karnac.

Hopkins, J. (1987). Failure of the holding relationship: Some effects of physical rejection on the child's attachment and his inner experience. *Journal of Child Psychotherapy, 13:* 5–17.

Hopkins, J. (1990). The observed infant of attachment theory. *British Journal of Psychotherapy, 6:* 460–470.

Hughes, D. (2005). Paper given at conference, "Out of control child: treating ADHD and other wild states without drugs or punishment". The Centre for Child Mental Health, London, 22 January.

Hunter, M., & Struve, J. (1997). *The Ethical Use of Touch in Psychotherapy.* London: Sage.

Hurry, A. (1998). Psychoanalysis and developmental therapy. In: A. Hurry (Ed.), *Psychoanalysis and Developmental Therapy* (pp. 32–73). London: Karnac.

Hutton, D. (1989). *Vogue,* Autumn.

International Psychoanalytic Association (2003). Telephone analysis: Seven practitioners give their views. *Insight* [supplement to the newsletter, *International Psychoanalysis*], 12: 13–32.

Jacoby, M. (1986). Getting in touch and touching in analysis. In: N. Schwartz-Salant & M. Stein (Eds.), *The Body in Analysis* (pp. 109–126). Wilmette, IL: Chiron.

Jacoby, R. (1986). *The Repression of Psychoanalysis: Otto Fenichel and the Political Freudians.* Chicago, IL: University of Chicago Press.

Johnson, D. H. (2000). Intricate tactile sensitivity. *Progress in Brain Research, 122:* 479–490.

Jones, P. (1996). *Drama as Therapy: Theatre as Living.* London: Routledge.

Juhane, D. (1987). *Job's Body: A Handbook for Bodywork*. Barrytown, NY: Station Hill.

Jung, C. G. (1931). Problems of modern psychotherapy. *C.W.*, *16*: 53–75, R. F. C. Hull (Trans.). London: Routledge & Kegan Paul.

Kahr, B. (1996). *D. W. Winnicott: A Biographical Portrait*. London: Karnac.

Klein, M. (1932). The sexual activities of children. In: *The Psycho-Analysis of Children* (pp. 111–120). London: Hogarth Press and the Institute of Psycho-Analysis, 1975.

Klein, M. (1957). Envy and gratitude. In: *Envy and Gratitude and Other Works 1946–1963* (pp. 176–235). London: Hogarth Press & the Institute of Psycho-Analysis, 1975.

Krueger, D. W. (1988). Body self, psychological self, and bulimia: Developmental and clinical considerations. In: H. J. Schwartz (Ed.), *Bulimia: Psychoanalytic Treatment and Theory* (pp. 55–72). Madison, CT: International Universities Press.

Langs, R. (1973). *The Technique of Psychoanalytic Psychotherapy. Volume 1: The Initial Contact, Theoretical Framework, Understanding the Patient's Communications, The Therapist's Interventions*. New York: Jason Aronson.

Langs, R. (1985). *Madness and Cure*. Lake Worth, FL: Gardner.

Langs, R. (1993). *Empowered Psychotherapy*. London: Karnac.

Langs, R. (1996). *The Evolution of the Emotion-processing Mind*. London: Karnac.

Langs, R. (1997). *Death Anxiety and Clinical Practice*. London: Karnac.

Langs, R. (1998). *Ground Rules in Psychotherapy and Counselling*. London: Karnac.

Langs, R. (2004a). *Fundamentals of Adaptive Psychotherapy and Counselling*. London: Palgrave-Macmillan.

Langs, R. (2004b). Death anxiety and the emotion-processing mind. *Psychoanalytic Psychology*, *21*: 31–53.

Langs, R., Badalamenti, A., & Thomson, L. (1996). *The Cosmic Circle: Unification of Mind, Matter and Energy*. Brooklyn, NY: Alliance.

Laplanche, J. (1970). *Life and Death in Psychoanalysis*. Baltimore, MD: Johns Hopkins University Press, 1976.

Laplanche, J., & Pontalis, J.-B. (1973). *The Language of Psychoanalysis*. London: Hogarth Press and the Institute of Psycho-Analysis.

Lazarus, A. (1994). How certain boundaries and ethics diminish therapeutic effectiveness. *Ethics and Behaviour*, *4*: 255–261.

Levine, P. A. (1997). *Waking the Tiger: Healing Trauma*. Berkeley, CA: North Atlantic.

Lévi-Strauss, C. (1963). *Structural Anthropology*. C. Jacobson & B. Schoepf (Trans.). New York: Basic Books.

Limentani, A. (1989). *Between Freud and Klein*. London: Free Association.

Lipton, S. D. (1977). Clinical observations on resistance to the transference. *International Journal of Psycho-Analysis*, 58: 463–472.

Little, M. (1966). Transference in borderline states. *International Journal of Psycho-Analysis*, 47: 476–485.

Little, M. I. (1985). Winnicott working in areas where psychotic anxieties predominate: a personal record. *Free Associations*, 1(3): 9–42. Also in: *Psychotic Anxieties and Containment: A Personal Record of an Analysis with Winnicott*. Northvale, NJ: Jason Aronson, 1990.

Lowen, A. (1967). *Betrayal of the Body*. New York: Macmillan.

McNeely, D. A. (1987). *Touching: Body Therapy and Depth Psychology*. Toronto: Inner City.

Menninger, K. (1958). *Theory of Psychoanalytic Technique*. New York: Basic Books.

Menzies-Lyth, I. (1988). *Containing Anxiety in Institutions: Selected Essays, Vol.1*. London: Free Association.

Merleau-Ponty, M. (1962). *Phenomenology of Perception*. C. Smith (Trans.). London: Routledge & Kegan Paul.

Meuser, K. T., Bellack, A. S., Douglas, M. S., & Morrison, R. L. (1991). Prevalence and stability of social skill deficits in schizophrenia. *Schizophrenia Research*, 5: 167–176.

Milner, M. (1969). *The Hands of the Living God: An Account of a Psycho-Analytic Treatment*. London: Hogarth.

Moberly, E. R. (1985). *The Psychology of Self and Other*. London: Tavistock.

Montagu, A. (1971). *Touching: The Human Significance of the Skin*. New York: Harper and Row.

Naitove, C. (1988). Using the arts therapies in treatment of sexual offenders against children. In: S. M. Sgroi (Ed.), *Vulnerable Populations, Vol. 1: Evaluation and Treatment of Sexually Abused Children and Adult Survivors* (pp. 265–298). Lexington, MA: Lexington Books.

Ogden, T. H. (1994). The analytic third: Working with intersubjective clinical facts. *International Journal of Psycho-Analysis*, 75: 3–19.

Orbach, S. (2003a). The John Bowlby Memorial Lecture 2003: Part I: There is no such thing as a body. *British Journal of Psychotherapy, 20*: 3–15. Also in: K. White (Ed.), *Touch: Attachment and the Body* (pp. 17–34). London: Karnac, 2004.

Orbach, S. (2003b). The John Bowlby Memorial Lecture 2003: Part II: Touch. *British Journal of Psychotherapy, 20*: 17–26. Also in: K. White (Ed.), *Touch: Attachment and the Body* (pp. 35–47). London: Karnac, 2004.

Padel, J. (1991). Interview with the author. 4th December.

Panksepp, J. (2003). Discussion. 4th International Neuro-Psychoanalysis Congress on The Unconscious in Cognitive Neuroscience and Psychoanalysis. July 25–28, New York.

Pedder, J. R. (1976). Attachment and new beginning: some links between the work of Michael Balint and John Bowlby. *International Review of Psycho-Analysis*, 3: 491–497 [reprinted in: G. Kohon (Ed.), *The British School of Psychoanalysis: The Independent Tradition* (pp. 295–308), London: Free Association, 1986].

Penn, D. L., & Meuser, K. T. (1996). Research update on the psychosocial treatment of schizophrenia. *American Journal of Psychiatry*, 153: 607–617.

Pinson, B. (2002). Touch in therapy: An effort to make the unknown known. *Journal of Contemporary Psychotherapy*, 32: 179–196.

Pozzi, M. E. (2003). The use of observation in the psychoanalytic treatment of a 12-year-old boy with Asperger's syndrome. *International Journal of Psychoanalysis*, 84: 1333–1349.

Prescott, J. W. (1971). Early somatosensory deprivation as an ontogenetic process in the abnormal development of the brain and behaviour. In: E. I. Goldsmith & J. Moor-Jankowski (Eds.), *Medical Primatology* (pp. 1–20). London: Karger.

Prescott, J. W. (1975). Body pleasure and the origins of violence. *Bulletin of Atomic Scientists*, November, pp. 10–20.

*Psychoanalytic Inquiry* (2000). *On Touch in the Psychoanalytic Situation*, 20: 1–186.

Reich, W. (1933). *Character Analysis*. V. Carfagno (Trans.). New York: Touchstone, 1972.

Reich, W. (1942). *The Function of the Orgasm*. London: Souvenir, 1983.

Rickman, J. (1947). Developments in psychoanalysis, 1896–1947. In: P. King (Ed.), *No Ordinary Psychoanalyst: The Exceptional Contributions of John Rickman* (pp. 71–84). London: Karnac, 2003.

Rodman, F. R. (2003). *Winnicott: Life and Work*. Oxford: Perseus.

Rosenfeld, H. (1947). Analysis of a schizophrenic state with depersonalization. *International Journal of Psycho-Analysis*, 28: 130–139.

Rosenfeld, H. (1949). Remarks on the relation of male homosexuality to paranoia, paranoid anxiety and narcissism. *International Journal of Psycho-Analysis*, 30: 36–47.

Rosenfeld, H. (1950). Note on the psychopathology of confusional states in chronic schizophrenias. *International Journal of Psycho-Analysis*, 31: 132–137.

Rosenfeld, H. (1952). Notes on the psycho-analysis of the super-ego conflict of an acute schizophrenic patient. *International Journal of Psycho-Analysis, 33*: 111–131.

Rosenzweig, M. R., Bennett, E. L., & Diamond, M. C. (1972). Brain changes in response to experience. *Scientific American, 226*(2): 22–29.

Rothschild, B. (2000). *The Body Remembers: The Psychophysiology of Trauma and Trauma Treatment*. New York: Norton.

Ruane, J. (2003). Sexuality in an institution. In: G. Adshead & C. Brown (Eds.), *Ethical Issues in Forensic Mental Health Research*. London: Jessica Kingsley.

Samuels, A. (1993). *The Political Psyche*. London: Routledge.

Schlesinger, H. J., & Appelbaum, A. H. (2000). When words are not enough. *Psychoanalytic Inquiry, 20*: 124–143.

Schore, A. N. (1994). *Affect Regulation and the Origin of the Self: The Neurobiology of Emotional Development*. Hillsdale, NJ: Lawrence Erlbaum.

Schore, A. N. (2001). Effects of a secure attachment relationship on right brain development, affect regulation, and infant mental health. *Infant Mental Health Journal, 22*: 7–66.

Segal, H. (1950). Some aspects of the analysis of a schizophrenic. *International Journal of Psycho-Analysis, 31*: 268–278.

Segal, H. (1956). Depression in the schizophrenic. *International Journal of Psycho-Analysis, 37*: 339–343.

Segal, H. (1979). Postscript 1979: The curative factors in psychoanalysis. In: *The Work of Hanna Segal: A Kleinian Approach to Clinical Practice* (pp. 79–80). New York: Jason Aronson, 1981.

Sharaf, M. (1983). *Fury on Earth: A Biography of Wilhelm Reich*. London: Hutchinson.

Sinason, V. (1988). Caught out. *Bradgate Poetry Press*, 4 May.

Sinason, V. (1992). *Mental Handicap and the Human Condition: New Approaches from the Tavistock*. London: Free Association Books.

Sinason, V. (1995). Interviews with Anne Marie Sandler and Arthur Couch. *Journal of Child Psychotherapy, 21*: 360–374.

Smith, D. L. (1989). An interview with Robert Langs. *Changes, 7*: 117–119.

Smith, D. L. (1991). *Hidden Conversations: An Introduction to Communicative Psychoanalysis*. London: Tavistock/Routledge.

Spitz, R. A. (1945). Hospitalism: An inquiry into the genesis of psychiatric conditions in early childhood. *The Psychoanalytic Study of the Child, 1*: 53–74.

Spitz, R. A. (1965). *The First Year of Life.* New York: International Universities Press.

Stern, D. N. (1990). *Diary of a Baby.* New York: Basic Books.

Stern, D. N., Sander, L. W., Nahum, J. P., Harrison, A. M., Lyons-Ruth, K., Morgan, A. C., Bruschweiler-Stern, N., & Tronick, E. Z. (1998). Non-interpretive mechanisms in psychoanalytic therapy: The "something more" than interpretation. *International Journal of Psycho-Analysis, 79*: 903–921.

Tarrier, N., Yusopoffs, F., Kinney, C., McCarthy, E., Gledhill, A., Haddock, G., & Morris, J. (1998). Randomised controlled trials of intensive cognitive behaviour therapy for patients with chronic schizophrenia. *British Medical Journal, 317*: 303–307.

Tausk, V. (1933). On the origin of the "influencing machine" in schizophrenia. *Psychoanalytic Quarterly, 2*: 519–556.

Totton, N. (1998). *The Water in the Glass: Body and Mind in Psychoanalysis.* London: Rebus.

Totton, N. (2003). *Body Psychotherapy: An Introduction.* Maidenhead: Open University Press.

Trevarthen, C. (1993). The self born in intersubjectivity: The psychology of an infant communicating. In: U. Neisser (Ed.), *The Perceived Self: Ecological and Interpersonal Sources of Self-Knowledge* (pp. 121–173). New York: Cambridge University Press.

Trevarthen, C., & Aitken, K. J. (2001). Infant intersubjectivity: research, theory and clinical applications. *Journal of Child Psychology and Psychiatry, 42*: 3–48.

Trevarthen, C., Aitken, K., Papoudi, D., & Robarts, J. (1996). *Children with Autism: Diagnosis and Interventions to Meet their Needs* (2nd edn). London: Jessica Kingsley.

Tune, D. (2005). Dilemmas around the ethical use of touch in psychotherapy. In: N. Totton (Ed.), *New Dimensions in Body Psychotherapy* (pp. 70–83). Maidenhead: Open University Press.

Tustin, F. (1972). *Autism and Childhood Psychosis.* London: Hogarth.

Tustin, F. (1981). *Autistic States in Children.* London: Routledge and Kegan Paul.

Walker, E., & Young, P. D. (1986). *A Killing Cure.* New York: Henry Holt.

Winnicott, D. W. (1954a). Play in the analytic situation. In C. Winnicott, R. Shepherd, & M. Davis (Eds.), *Psycho-Analytic Explorations* (pp. 28–29). London: Karnac, 1989.

Winnicott, D. W. (1954b). Letter to W. Clifford M. Scott, 27th January. In: F. R. Rodman (Ed.), *The Spontaneous Gesture: Selected Letters of*

*D. W. Winnicott* (pp. 56–57). Cambridge, MA: Harvard University Press, 1987.

Winnicott, D. W. (1955). Metapsychological and clinical aspects of regression within the psycho-analytical set-up. *International Journal of Psycho-Analysis, 36*: 16–26 [reprinted in: *Through Paediatrics to Psycho-Analysis: Collected Papers* (pp. 278–294), London: Karnac, 1992].

Winnicott, D. W. (1957). On the contribution of direct child observation to psycho-analysis. In: *The Maturational Processes and the Facilitating Environment: Studies in the Theory of Emotional Development* (pp. 109–114). London: Hogarth Press & The Institute of Psycho-Analysis, 1965.

Winnicott, D. W. (1960). The theory of the parent–infant relationship. *International Journal of Psycho-Analysis, 41*: 585–595.

Winnicott, D. W. (1963). Psychiatric disorder in terms of infantile maturational processes. In: *The Maturational Processes and the Facilitating Environment: Studies in the Theory of Emotional Development* (pp. 230–241). London: Hogarth Press & The Institute of Psycho-Analysis, 1965.

Winnicott, D. W. (1967a). Letter to Charles Clay Dahlberg, 24 October. In: F. R. Rodman (Ed.), *The Spontaneous Gesture: Selected Letters of D. W. Winnicott* (pp. 171–172). Cambridge, MA: Harvard University Press, 1987.

Winnicott, D. W. (1967b). Mirror-role of mother and family in child development. In: *Playing and Reality* (pp. 111–118). London: Tavistock, 1971.

Winnicott, D. W. (1971). Playing: a theoretical statement. In: *Playing and Reality* (pp. 38–52). London: Tavistock.

# INDEX

abstinence and neutrality, 16, 20, 29
    51–53, 73, 111, 113–115, 142
abuse, 11, 45, 73–74, 150, 157, 172,
    175
  child, 56, 158, 163, 172
    sexual, 7, 43, 52, 69–71, 92,
    112–113, 117–119
    ritual, 57–58, 76
  drug, 101
  emotional, 50
  physical, xxiii, 50, 69, 71, 112, 117,
    174
  POPAN—the Prevention of
    Professional Abuse Network,
    52
  psychological, 69, xxiii
  sexual, xxiii, 47, 55, 170, 174
acting out, 73, 102–103, 114, 117,
    122, 127, 132, 174
adolescent(s), 69, 109, 112, 114–115,
    121–122
affect(s)/affective, xvii–xviii, 15, 19,
    80, 86, 88, 90–91, 96

auto-, 89–91, 95
aggression/aggressive, 101, 110,
    116, 148, 169–170
Aitken, K. J., 90, 159, 187
American Psychoanalytic
    Association, 11
Anderson, J. W., 10, 179
anonymous questionnaire(s), xvi
anthropology/anthropologists,
    xxiii, 51, 166
anxiety, 18, 48, 73, 105, 121,
    126–127, 131, 152, 173–174
  death, xxiv, 128–131, 135–136, 139
  performance, 170
  separation, 25
  sexual, 106
Anzieu, D., 85–86, 89, 92, 179
Appelbaum, A. H., 111, 186
asylums in Leros, Greece, 56–57
attachment, 86, 90, 136
  figures, 74, 171
  relations/behaviour, 42, 91–92,
    94, 96, 171

theory, xxiii, 50, 171
attraction/attractive, 18, 118
autism, xxiii, 80, 88–90, 101, 109,
    115–116
auto-erotism/auto-erotic, 84

Badalamenti, A., 131, 183
Baker, E. F., 154, 179
Balint, M., xx, 16, 23–24, 30–31,
    40–42, 179
Barnes, B., 170, 179
Bellack, A. S., 164, 184
Bennett, E. L., 101, 186
Benthien, C., 83, 86, 179
Bick, E., 85–86, 114, 179
body, xviii, xxiii, 3–5, 9, 18, 23, 26,
    32, 34–37, 39, 41, 43, 46, 51, 55,
    59, 67, 69–75, 77, 82–85, 87, 89,
    93, 97, 99, 101, 103–108,
    115–116, 118–120, 146–147,
    172–174
    and brain/mind processes, 90, 94,
    106
    hatred, 74, 77, 99–100, 107
    image, 101, 104
    memory, 86–87
    self, 23
    space, 90
    therapy/therapist(s), xiii, xviii,
    xxi, xxiv, 31, 59, 93, 145–147,
    150–155, 157–161
borderline, 1, 116, 151
boundaries, xxiv, 1–3, 6–7, 9–10, 13,
    25, 32, 34, 47–48, 52, 72, 81, 98,
    100, 103, 105, 114, 119, 128–129,
    133, 146, 160, 167, 169–170, 172
    bodily/physical, 73–74, 81, 98,
    119, 146, 173, 177
    generational, 115
    of consensual touch, 168
Bowlby, J., xx, 42, 171, 179
breast/breast-feeding/milk, 9, 11,
    31–32, 88
Briggs, A., 114, 179
Bruschweiler-Stern, N., 75, 187
Bryan, K., 164, 180

Carroll, R., 59, 93–94, 180
case histories
    Anne, 69–72
    Carole, 55–56
    Joan, 53–55
    Maureen, 58–59
    Mavis, 31–38
    Mr Edwards, 137–138
    Sarah, 57
    traumatized child, 66–69
Casement, P., xxi, 7–8, 16, 23–24, 73,
    76, 111, 149, 180
children, xiii, xxii–xxiii, 1, 24, 39, 43,
    52, 66, 109–112, 114–117,
    120–122, 163, 172 see also:
    adolescents
    autistic, 89, 115
    of Romania, 56
    offenders against, 179
    physical violence of, 19
    psychotic, 10, 115
    with developmental deficits, 121
    with eating disorders, 100
    with learning disabilities, 50, 109
code of ethics, 47
Conger, J. P., 157, 159, 180
conscious/deep unconscious
    systems, 3, 124 126–133,
    138–143
    deep unconscious fear of death,
    130
    deep unconscious wisdom, 125,
    128–129, 133, 136, 142
    morality and ethics, 129–130
couch, 1, 3–4, 11, 17, 21, 27, 34, 50,
    54, 56–59, 67, 97, 104, 108, 121
countertransference, xv–xvi, xviii,
    18, 30, 52, 72, 91, 101, 112, 119,
    155–156, 167
    erotic, 95, 160

Davies, J. M., 76, 180
Decobert, S., 10, 180
deep unconscious systems, see
    conscious/deep unconscious
    sytems

defence(s), xvii, xxiv, xxiv, 37, 43,
    59, 101, 124–125, 127, 129, 132,
    139, 170, 173, 175
    autistic, 90
Denman, C., 150, 180
Derrida, J., 85, 180
development, 23, 38–40, 42, 73, 84,
    86, 93, 96, 121–122, 171
    and touch, 39, 90–91, 96, 101, 174
    see also: developmental delay,
    developmental psychology,
    developmental therapy
    sexual, 12
developmental delay, xxiii, 109, 168
    see also: development
developmental psychology, xxiii,
    51, 86 see also: development,
    developmental delay,
    developmental therapy
developmental therapy, 121 see also:
    development, developmental
    delay, developmental
    psychology
Diamond, N., 92, 101, 180
disability, xxii–xxiii, 53, 55, 109,
    115
dissociative identity disorder, 58–59
Dockar-Drysdale, B., 10–11, 180
Douglas, M. S., 164, 184
dream(s), 8–9, 111, 124–125, 130,
    135, 138, 142
    day, 66
    erotic, 106
drive(s), 114, 173
    pleasure-seeking, 42
    aggressive and sexual, 29 see also:
    libido

eating disorders, 99–101
    anorexia, xxiii
    bulimia, xxiii, 99–100, 104
ego, 33, 41, 47, 73, 94, 128, 156,
    170
    skin, 83, 86
Eigen, M., 157, 180
Eissler, K. R., 10, 180

Embodied–Relational Therapy,
    155–157 see also: body:
    therapy/therapist(s)
emotion-processing mind, 125–129,
    132, 142
Ernst, S., 170, 179
erotic, 3, 96, 102, 159–160
    auto-, 84
    caress, 82
    dream, 106
    intimacy, 95
    love, 95
    presence of the, 101
    relationships, 175
    response/impulse, 159
    sense of self, 176

fantasy/phantasy, 4, 7, 12, 32–33,
    35–38, 44, 95, 101, 105, 111, 127,
    151, 160, 170
Farrell, E., 100, 180
Federn, P., 85, 180
fellatio, 17–18
Ferenczi, S., xx, 3, 30–31, 52, 148,
    157–158, 181
forensic therapist(s)/
    psychotherapeutic practice,
    xxi, xxiv, 163–177
    drama therapy, 166–169
    sex offenders in, 170–171
Forer, B. R., 101–102, 181
Frank, L. K., 39, 181
free association, xix, 1, 3, 64, 66, 80,
    125, 152, 156
Freud, A., 121
Freud, S., xix, 1, 3, 16, 20–21, 23,
    29–31, 50–52, 64–66, 80, 84, 88,
    91, 101, 126, 148, 157, 181
Freudian(s), 16, 29–30, 42, 45, 146

Gabbard, G. O., 52, 181
Gledhill, A., 164, 187
good enough mothering/holding,
    47, 142
Gramsci, A., 82, 181
Greene, A. U., 31, 181

Grosskurth, P., 148, 181
guided association, 125, 130
Guntrip, H., 17, 49, 181

Haddock, G., 164, 187
Hale, R., 76, 182
hand(s), 2–4, 14, 20, 29, 31, 33–37,
    51, 54, 56, 59, 67, 83–85, 98–99,
    104, 112, 118, 138, 152–153, 161,
    172
  and mouth, 31, 33, 58
  -holding, 2–3, 5, 8–10, 12–13, 16,
    19, 23–24, 26, 35–37, 42, 45–46,
    50, 73, 103, 110–111, 115–116,
    120–121, 137–138, 148–151
  shake(s), 3, 6–7, 16–17, 24, 26, 50,
    56–57, 62–64, 69, 71, 73, 103,
    106, 109–110, 115, 129–130, 166,
    168
Harrison, A. M., 75, 187
Hawkins, P., 167, 182
Henton, R., 165, 182
hierarchy of the senses, 82–82, 91
Hoffer, W., 33–34, 182
Holder, A., 110, 114, 116, 121, 182
Hopkins, J., 171, 174
Hughes, D., 115, 182
Hunter, M., 50, 148, 182
Hurry, A., 121, 182
Hutton, D., 100, 182
Hyde, K., 170, 179

incest taboo, 81
inhibitions/prohibitions on touch
  in a high-security environment,
    164, 166
  in society, 43
  in the analytic setting, 47, 79–81,
    83, 89, 98, 101
International Psychoanalytic
  Association, 182
interpretation(s), xvi–xvii, 10–11,
    13, 17, 19, 24–26, 40, 45, 47,
    75–77, 103, 111, 117, 119, 124,
    132, 139

Jacoby, M., 30–31, 44, 149, 182
Jacoby, R., 145, 182
Johnson, D. H., 153, 182
Jones, P., 167, 182
Juhane, D., 147, 183
Jung, C. G., 30, 42, 183
Jungian, 29–31, 45

Kahr, B., 1, 6, 183
Kinney, C., 164, 187
kiss-punch, 52
Klein, M., 27, 51, 67, 73, 105, 183
Kleinian, 102
Krueger, D. W., 101, 183

Langs, R., 3, 6–7, 9, 123, 128,
    131–133, 136, 139, 141–142, 183
Laplanche, J., 75, 84, 183
Lazarus, A., 49, 183
Levine, P. A., 157, 183
Lévi-Strauss, C., 81, 184
libido, 29–30
  and aggression/sex, 29–30
  and religion, 30
Limentani, A., 184
linguistics, xxiii, 51, 86, 87, 96
Lipton, S. D., 12, 184
Little, M., 5–6, 9–10, 12–13, 16, 30,
    40–41, 47, 116, 149, 153, 184
Lowen, A., 44, 184
Lyons-Ruth, K., 75, 187

Marrone, M., 92, 180
massage, 44, 50, 98–100, 102–103,
    106–107, 154–155
McCarthy, E., 164, 187
McNeely, D. A., 145, 184
Menninger, K., 50, 184
Menzies-Lyth, I., 173, 184
Merleau-Ponty, M., 84–85, 88, 184
message analysing centre (MAC),
    126–127, 130
Meuser, K. T., 164, 184–185
Milner, M., 106–107, 184
mirroring, 72–73, 77, 84–85, 104,
    146, 160

Moberly, E. R., 10, 184
Montagu, A., 147, 184
Morgan, A. C., 75, 187
Morris, J., 164, 187
Morrison, R. L., 164, 184
mother/carer–baby relationship,
    42, 157, 159

Nahum, J. P., 75, 187
Naitove, C., 168, 184
narcissism, 84
narrative(s), 72, 124–125, 129, 131,
    133, 135, 138, 140–143, 169
    non-, 125, 130
neurophysiology/neurobiology,
    89–91
neuroscience, xxiii, 41, 51, 86, 90, 93,
    159
neurosis, xvii, 65
non-erotic, 6, 101
non-verbal communication, 15, 19,
    25, 86, 110–111, 156, 165,
    169–170

object, 19, 33, 41, 84, 92, 107, 112,
    121–122
    relations, 30, 42
Ogden, T. H., 95, 184
oral contact, 23
Orbach, S., xx, 23, 50, 74, 99, 103,
    167, 184
orphanage babies and touch, 50, 91
osteopathy, 155
    cranial, 59

Padel, J., 3–4, 195
Panksepp, J., 90, 185
Papoudi, D., 90,187
Pedder, J. R., 16, 42, 185
Penn, D. L., 164, 185
phenomenology, xxiii, 84
physical handicap, 117–120
Pinson, B., 102, 185
play/playing, 59, 66, 114, 116, 122,
    167, 169, 175
Pontalis, J.-B., 84, 183

Pozzi, M. E., 117, 185
Prescott, J. W., 101, 147, 185
pressure technique, xix, 3, 80
pre-verbal
    communication, 39, 41, 86
    disturbances, 44
primal scream, 24
projective identification, 113, 173
Psychoanalytic Inquiry, 16, 23, 185
psychoanalytic theory, xvi, 83

reflexology, 59
regression/regressive, xvii, 4–5,
    10–13, 15, 17–18, 20, 23–24,
    40–42, 47–48, 102–103, 116, 140,
    149, 157–160, 169
Reich, W., 44, 145–146, 150, 154, 157,
    185
Reichian, 145, 154–155
repression, 44, 127, 156
Rickman, J., 64–66, 185
Robarts, J., 90, 187
Rodman, F. R., 18, 185
Rosenfeld, E., 27
Rosenfeld, H., 12, 185–186
Rosenzweig, M. R., 101, 186
Rothschild, B., 146, 157, 186
Ruane, J., 176, 186

Samuels, A., 160, 186
Sander, L. W., 75, 187
Schlesinger, H. J., 111, 186
Schore, A. N., 86, 91, 159, 186
Searles, H., xx
Segal, H., 11–12, 186
self–other relation, 84, 91, 95
setting(s), xvi, 9, 11, 44, 66, 96, 114,
    130, 134
    cultural, 62–63
    forensic, 163–166, 171, 173–177
        physical contact in, 171–175
        touching between patients in,
        175–176
    group, 95, 165, 171
Sharaf, M., 150, 186
Shohet, R., 167, 182

Sideras, V., 165, 182
Sinason, V., 51, 53, 76, 118, 182, 186
Sinclair, R., 165, 182
skin, 8, 23, 42–43, 70, 75, 79, 83,
    85–88, 90, 92, 152
    ego, 83, 86
    grafts, 71
Smith, D. L., 3, 7, 9, 13, 186
social skills, 164–165
Spitz, R. A., 34, 50, 186–187
split, split off, 51, 94, 102, 170
Stern, D. N., 42, 75, 187
strong adaptive (communicative)
    approach, xxiv, 123–124, 126,
    130, 132–133, 135–136, 143
Struve, J., 50, 148, 182
superego, 50

talking cure, 20, 81–82, 115
Tarrier, N., 164, 187
Tausk, V., 92, 187
telephone analysis, 22
therapist–patient relationship, xvi,
    17, 30, 42, 48, 63–64, 66, 73, 75,
    80, 91, 94, 98, 114–115, 117, 145,
    155–156, 158, 160, 167, 171–172
    sexual/sexualized, xx, 17, 19, 45,
    48, 52, 73, 159
Thomson, L., 131, 183
Totton, N., 146, 154, 187
touch and breath, 155–156
touch as amplification, 153–154
touch as comfort, 147–152, 156
touch as provocation, 154
touch as skilled intervention, 155
    acupressure, 155
    craniosacral therapy, 155
    massage, 155

osteopathy, 155
shiatsu, 155
touch to explore contact, 152–153,
    156
transference, xxii–xxiii, 1, 17, 23, 25,
    27, 50, 60, 64–66, 94, 100, 108,
    111–112, 116, 118, 120, 134, 148,
    155–156, 167
    erotic, 95
    figures/object, 121
    negative, 116
trauma(s), xxii, 7–9, 16–17, 23–24,
    43, 50, 52, 55, 58–59, 66, 70,
    73, 75, 90, 111, 126, 135–136,
    140, 147, 149, 157–158,
    172–174
    retraumatization, 157
Trevarthen, C., 86, 90, 159, 187
trigger decoding, 129–131, 133, 135,
    140
Tronick, E. Z., 75, 187, 187
Tune, D., 148, 187
Tustin, F., 88–90, 187

unheimlich, 91–92

violence, 19, 101, 105, 117, 136, 140,
    147, 163, 167, 173

Walker, E., 11, 187
Winnicott, D. W., xx, xxii–xxiii, 1–6,
    9–19, 23, 26, 30–31, 40, 42, 51,
    66–67, 71, 74, 116, 149, 157, 167,
    187–188
Winnicottian, 7

Young, P. D., 11, 187
Yusopoffs, F., 164, 187